A MANUAL ON WRITING RESEARCH

REVISED

by

KATHLEEN DUGDALE

A MANUAL ON

WRITING RESEARCH

Revised

by

KATHLEEN DUGDALE

Editor of Publications in Education
Indiana University

BLOOMINGTON, INDIANA

1967

TMLC

PE
1478
D8
1967

Copyright © 1962, 1967 by
KATHLEEN DUGDALE

Published by the Author
FOR SALE BY
THE INDIANA UNIVERSITY BOOKSTORE
Bloomington, Indiana

Try LC

PREFACE

As its name suggests, *A Manual on Writing Research* is designed as a reference book for persons who are conducting and reporting research studies, and especially for those who are writing the research report. It is planned as a companion book to *A Manual of Form for Theses and Term Reports,* which has been in use for several years.

Of the two manuals, the present one is naturally the one which will be needed first by the research writer, but the manual on form is also very important, as it concerns the typographical form of the final typed report. Duplication of information between the two manuals has been held to a minimum, with the points that would necessarily be included in both being elaborated on in the one in which the writer would most often need the information and being merely generalized in the other manual.

In gathering material for the *Manual on Writing Research,* a great many reference books were consulted, the majority of which were in the field of either research or rhetoric and grammar. As a help to the student needing more information in these fields, a few of the best reference books have been listed in a bibliography at the end of the manual. An attempt was made to select, from the vast amount of material collected, the suggestions that would be most valuable to persons writing reports in any field of research and to present them in logical order.

Since it is assumed that a person undertaking to do research is already well informed concerning elementary rhetoric and grammar, the help given in these fields concerns, for the most part, the more advanced or the less often used material.

For several years before writing this manual, the author kept notes on the questions asked by doctoral candidates writing their theses and on the errors found in theses and other research materials she was editing for publication. These notes have served as a tentative guide in determining the kind of material that beginning research writers would find most useful in a book of this kind.

The author is deeply appreciative of the help received from those who generously gave of their time and thought to reading the completed manuscript and who offered valuable criticisms and constructive suggestions. She is especially indebted to Dr. Clinton I. Chase, Associate Professor of Education and Associate Director of the Bureau of Educational Studies and Testing; Dr. Nicholas A. Fattu, Research Professor of Education and Director of the Institute of Educational Research; Dr. Carolyn Guss, Professor of Education and Associate in Selection of Audio-Visual Materials; Dr. H. Glenn Ludlow, Professor of Education and Director of the Bureau of Educational Studies and Testing; and Dr. Richard Lee Turner, Professor of Education, all of whom are faculty members at Indiana University and are well versed in research methods. These individuals have not only carried on studies of their own but have directed many research studies and doctoral theses as well.

To these and to all others who contributed in any way to the progress and completion of this manual, the author wishes to express her sincere thanks.

K.D.

TABLE OF CONTENTS

Introduction 1

The Preliminaries 2

Selecting the Topic 2

    Selecting the field of study 2
    Selecting the research problem 2
    Limiting the problem 2

Planning the Study 2

    Writing a preliminary outline 2
    Writing a proposal 3

The Gathering and Handling of the Data 4

Reading Extensively and Taking Notes 4

    Locating materials in the library 4
    Taking notes 6
    Filing notes 7

Gathering and Checking Data Obtained from Others 7

Using and Developing Data-Gathering Tools 9

    Writing letters requesting information 9
    Preparing pencil-and-paper instruments 9
    Developing questionnaires and opinionnaires 10
    Using standardized tests and other measuring devices 11
    Seeking information through interviews 11
    Seeking information through observation 12

Handling the Data 12

The Writing of the Research Report 14

Outlining the Final Study 14

Writing the First Draft 15

    Providing good working conditions 15
    Thinking through the problem 15
    Writing the introduction 15
    Writing the review of related research 16
    Quoting from other studies 16
    Including footnotes 16
    Writing the body of the report 17
    Including illustrative materials 18
    Writing the concluding chapter 18
    Making up the supplementary pages 19

Revising the Report 20

SUGGESTIONS FOR CLEAR AND EFFECTIVE WRITING	21
Making the Report Rhetorically Correct	21
Making the Report Grammatically Correct	22
Using good sentence structure	22
Using parallel constructions	23
Listing items in series	23
Placing prepositions at the end of a sentence	23
Stating comparisons clearly	23
Using pronouns properly	24
Using possessives correctly	24
Using correct verb forms	24
Selecting Appropriate Vocabulary	26
Using Correct Spelling and Capitalization	26
Forming plurals	27
Forming possessives	27
Hyphenating	27
Abbreviating	27
Expressing numbers	28
Capitalizing correctly	28
Using Correct Punctuation	28
TROUBLESOME WORDS AND CONSTRUCTIONS	33
BIBLIOGRAPHY	45
INDEX	47

INTRODUCTION

Research is an honest, intensive, and purposeful search for facts and principles that throw new light on a subject. Before attempting to do a piece of research, one must have a general understanding of what is involved in making a study of this kind and in reporting the findings. The present manual is designed to help those who are not thoroughly acquainted with these matters and who are seeking information on the subject.

A Manual on Writing Research is merely a series of suggestions to guide research writers. While it cannot cover all the points that come up in writing research, it does include most of those that arise repeatedly, both in the more extensive kinds of studies, such as independent research and doctoral theses, and in the less involved and shorter studies required for term reports. The suggestions given are combined and condensed in order that as many points as possible may be covered, and therefore they should be read especially carefully and thoughtfully. They are presented in logical order (for the most part in the order in which the research writer will have need of them) and are numbered consecutively so that they can be located readily when looked up in the index.

Much has been written to assist the researcher in selecting and limiting his problem, planning his study, and securing and handling his data. Consequently, it was felt that many of the topics that are normally included in a book on research need be touched upon here only lightly. An attempt has been made, however, to cover all those points which might be particularly needed by beginning research writers in any field and especially by students working on theses and research reports. Detailed suggestions concerning many phases of research can be found in the references listed in the bibliography (page 45).

The most important ingredients in a well written research report are good organization of material and effective use of the English language. To achieve the first of these, the making of an outline is essential, as it gives one the opportunity to see a skeleton of the report. Because of the brevity of an outline, poor organization, duplication of material, or lack of material needed to make the report clear can be noted rather quickly. The outline may have to be revised often as the writing progresses, but it should always be available as a guide. Planning and filling in this framework of the study and carefully revising the written report are phases of good presentation that take a great deal of time and intensive reflective thinking.

But good organization alone does not guarantee a well written report. Although it is assumed that a person attempting to report research has a thorough understanding of the elementary rules of rhetoric, it is recommended that he review his rhetoric and grammar, so that he will know how to give his study unity, coherence, emphasis, and clarity.

Research writing is formal writing, and the use of conversational or informal English for such a purpose is considered incorrect. Many points in English usage may seem minor, but to the research writer they are important because it is essential that he express the exact meaning he wishes to convey. The emphasis, here, is placed on the technique of putting words together into effective sentences, of weaving sentences into logical paragraphs, and of combining paragraphs into well planned chapters. It is hoped that students will find most of the answers to their questions in this manual.

Many puzzling or unusual words or constructions are encountered when attempting to make statements correct and clear. Suggestions as to the preferred forms and uses of troublesome words and constructions are given on pages 33 to 44. This list is by no means all-inclusive. Most of the more commonly used items have been omitted on the assumption that the educational background of the research writer has given him knowledge of these.

After the research report has been written and the revisions made, it must be typed in good form if it is to give evidence that it has been made with care. Since no study can look its best unless the form is consistent and since consistency is not possible without rules, it is recommended that the rules in a detailed stylebook be followed. The companion book to the present manual (*A Manual of Form for Theses and Term Reports*) is recommended as one which, if carefully followed, will help make the report both correct and attractive typographically.

It is hoped that the suggestions offered in both of these manuals will prove helpful to all who have need of them.

THE PRELIMINARIES

Selecting the Topic

Selecting the field of study

1. Discuss the subject of a research topic with people who are informed in the field of research, and seek suggestions from them.
2. Select a field of study in which you are interested and open-minded and in which you can find sufficient information.
3. Select a field which your experience, skills, and training qualify you to undertake.
4. Become acquainted with the factors involved, the difficulties to be encountered, and the special conditions required in carrying on research in the field.
5. Locate the studies in the library or elsewhere that have been made in the field, and read the prefaces, tables of contents, and other headings in some of these books.
6. Read more carefully those references that seem to be the most important and that promise to be of the greatest help to you in carrying on a study in the field, and take notes on these.
7. List in a temporary bibliography all references you find that are related to the field.

Selecting the research problem

8. After determining the general field of study in which you think you would like to do your research, select a problem in that field which is timely, important, and, preferably, of more than local significance.
9. Select (a) a problem which needs further investigation, (b) one whose solution would fill a gap in present investigations, or (c) one which can be used as a basis for future research.
10. Select a problem which can be solved with the subjects, library facilities, techniques, equipment, and working conditions available.
11. Select a problem for which you can get sponsorship and cooperation.
12. Select a problem which is related to your career and which does not involve physical, social, or professional risks, or great expense in either time or money.
13. Do not select a problem about which you are prejudiced or in which you are emotionally involved.

Limiting the problem

14. Before beginning to collect the data or plan the study, limit it as to subjects, situations, geographical areas, materials, and so forth, so that it can be treated exhaustively.
15. Break down the limits of each area, progressively, until the problem is of manageable proportions. For example, if you plan to study salaries of secretaries, you might break down the subject into salaries of private secretaries, salaries of those in industrial concerns, of those in industrial concerns in Chicago, of those in industrial concerns in Chicago in 1967, etc.
16. After you have sufficiently limited the problem state it simply and clearly and define its limits, using specific terms.

Planning the Study

17. Skim several of the better known books dealing with your topic in order to get the feel of the material.
18. Determine what has already been done in the field and what is still to be done.
19. As you become aware of the points you should cover in your study and of the material that should be included under them, record them.
20. Determine (a) the kind of data needed, (b) the source and availability of the data, (c) the methods and techniques that seem appropriate for collecting and handling the data, and (d) the relative importance of both internal and external validity.

Writing a preliminary outline

21. Use your reference material to develop a preliminary outline before doing any detailed reading.

22. Follow the general pattern of organization used in most research studies unless your study is such that it must be handled differently. This pattern includes three main divisions: (a) the introduction, (b) the body, and (c) the conclusions, with each division containing one or more chapters and most chapters containing subdivisions.

23. Word the topical headings so that they are meaningful, and set them up so that the levels of headings indicate the relationship of the topics to one another.

24. From a careful study of this outline, decide definitely whether or not you can get the materials necessary and whether or not you are interested in undertaking the study.

25. Use this preliminary outline as a guide in taking additional notes, organizing the data, and preparing to write the proposal.

Writing a proposal

26. If from your outline you decide you wish to undertake the proposed research, write a proposal, or tentative report, of what you propose to do and of how you propose to do it.

27. Give the study a temporary, clearly stated and fairly specific title. This can be, and probably will be, changed as the study progresses.

28. Tell how you happened to become interested in the subject.

29. State the need for the study as you see it and the need as expressed by authorities in the field.

30. Tell how you think the findings can be of value in helping solve the problem.

31. In the introduction, state the problem clearly and point out its limitations.

32. Give a brief account of the background of the study.

33. Give a clear, concise statement of the major and minor problems you propose to solve.

34. Review the related research briefly.
    a. Criticize and analyze each reference you have read.
    b. Comment on each reference in relation to its style of presentation, the dependability of its data, the accuracy of its findings, and the logical drawing of its conclusions.
    c. Discuss a few studies in detail, describing their contribution to your study.

35. Describe the population to be used and the way in which it is to be selected.

36. Use appropriate representative subjects that are available in sufficient number to be reliable.

37. Describe the kind of data needed, the source of the data, and how the data can be collected.

38. Gather preliminary data and read literature before setting up hypotheses.

39. Determine your basic assumptions—assumptions that the sample is representative of the total population, that the subjects are qualified to give the information you are seeking, that the way in which you propose to collect the data is appropriate for the purpose, etc.

40. Set up reasonable hypotheses through inference to guide in the development of the study and to facilitate the solution of the problem. These should be clearly related to the problem statement. (Hypotheses suggest the answers to questions that arise or to problems to be solved concerning what, when, where, who, and why. They are not essential in all research presentations but are a valuable addition. They can be in affirmative or question form, but they can be checked statistically more easily if they are stated in negative form.)

41. Justify the hypotheses on the basis of authority, experience, or the results expected.

42. If more than one hypothesis is included, show the relationship of these to one another.

43. Describe the methods and tools to be used to test the hypotheses or answer the objectives.

44. Define all technical terms, and any other terms used with a special meaning.

45. Present logically and systematically the topics and subtopics which you plan to discuss in the study.
    a. Explain how the data would be classified and analyzed.
    b. Name the data-gathering devices to be used.

46. Describe the way in which the data are to be presented when analyzed.

47. Propose methods that will insure the validity and reliability of the data.

48. In the organization of the report, do not divide the study under too many headings.

49. Suggest the possible conclusions to be drawn from the study and the applications that might be made of the findings.

50. Include a bibliography of the references that have helped you decide upon the topic and method proposed.

THE GATHERING AND HANDLING OF THE DATA

Reading Extensively and Taking Notes

51. If from your outline and proposal, your problem seems feasible and promising and you are interested in studying it more intensively, begin by reading all the material you can find on the subject.

Locating materials in the library

52. Locate the various guides to materials in your field. The card catalog will tell you which materials are in the library. Some of the best known are as follows:

GENERAL GUIDES

Books in Print, H. W. Wilson Co., Inc., New York, 1928-.
Education Index, H. W. Wilson Co., Inc., New York, 1929-.
Essay and General Literature Index, H. W. Wilson Co., Inc., New York, 1900-.
Paperbound Books in Print, R. R. Bowker Co., New York, 1955-.
Subject Guide to Books in Print, R. R. Bowker Co., New York, 1957-.
United States Catalog: Books in Print, 1899-1928 (now *Cumulative Book Index,* H. W. Wilson Co., Inc., New York, 1928-).

PERIODICALS AND NEWSPAPERS

Poole's Index to Periodical Literature, Houghton Mifflin Co., Boston, 1882-1908.
New Serial Titles, Library of Congress, U.S. Library of Congress, Washington, D.C., 1950-.
New York Times Index, New York Times, New York, 1913-.
Public Affairs Information Service Bulletin, Public Affairs Information Service, New York, 1915-.
Readers' Guide to Periodical Literature, H. W. Wilson Co., Inc., New York, 1901-.
Social Sciences and Humanities Index, H. W. Wilson Co., Inc., New York, 1907-.
Ulrich's International Periodicals Directory, R. R. Bowker Co., New York, vol. 1, 1965; vol. 2, 1966.
Union List of Serials, H. W. Wilson Co., Inc., New York, 1927-1949.

ENCYCLOPEDIAS

Encyclopedia Americana, Americana Corporation, New York, 1964, 30 vols.
Encyclopaedia Britannica, Encyclopaedia Britannica, Inc., Chicago, 1964, 24 vols.
Encyclopedia of Educational Research, The Macmillan Co., London, 1960, 1564 pp.
Special encyclopedias in many fields—business, drama, education, engineering, home economics, radio, religion, science, sports, etc.

DICTIONARIES

A Dictionary of Modern English Usage, by Henry Watson Fowler, Clarendon Press, Oxford, 1965, 725 pp.
Funk and Wagnalls New Standard Dictionary, Funk and Wagnalls, 1959, 2815 pp.
International Thesaurus, by Peter M. Roget, Thomas W. Crowell Co., New York, 1962.
The Random House Dictionary of the English Language, Random House, Inc., New York, 1966.
Webster's Third New International Dictionary, G. C. Merriam Co., Springfield, Massachusetts, 1961, 2662 pp.

Humbray, Harold H.
The Use of Test Scores
Brown Bros., N.Y., 1961
175 pp.

LB1042
I. U. Lib.

Based on data gathered by questionnaire
Used only 25 cases

A MANUAL ON WRITING RESEARCH

Webster's Dictionary of Synonyms, G. C. Merriam Co., Springfield, Massachusetts, 1942, 907 pp.
Special dictionaries in special fields such as occupations, art, etc.

BIOGRAPHIES
Current Biography, H. W. Wilson Co., Inc., New York, 1940-.
Who's Who in America, Marquis, Chicago, 1899-.

BIBLIOGRAPHIES
The Bibliographic Index, H. W. Wilson Co., Inc., New York, 1938-.
Bibliographies in special fields such as agriculture, art, music, psychology, etc.

GOVERNMENT PUBLICATIONS
United Nations Documents Index, United Nations, New York, 1950-.
United States Government Publication, U. S. Superintendent of Documents, Washington, D.C., 1895-.
Material from various local governmental agencies includes official reports, research studies, documents, statistical data, laws, etc.

DIRECTORIES
Ayer and Son's Directory of Newspapers and Periodicals, N. A. Ayer and Son, Philadelphia, 1880-.
Educational Directory, U. S. Office of Education, Washington, D.C., 1912-.

ALMANACS AND YEARBOOKS
Facts on File, Facts on File, Inc., New York, 1940-.
Information Please Almanac, Simon and Schuster, New York, 1947-.
Statesman's Yearbook, The Macmillan Co., London, 1864-.
The World Almanac, and Book of Facts, The World Almanac Division, Newspaper Enterprises Association, New York, 1868-.

ATLASES AND GAZETTEERS
Atlas of American History, by James T. Adams, Charles Scribner's Sons, New York, 1943, 360 pp.
Hammond's Universal World Atlas, C. S. Hammond, New York, 1956.

Rand McNally Cosmopolitan World Atlas, Rand McNally and Co., New York, 1964, 124 pp.

THESES
Dissertation Abstracts (formerly *Microfilm Abstracts*, 1938-1952), University Microfilms, Ann Arbor, Michigan, 1953-.

MICROFILMS, MICROFORMS, AND AUDIO-VISUAL AIDS
Guide to Free Tapes, Scripts, and Transcriptions, Educators Progress Service, Randolph, Wisconsin.
Library of Congress: Motion Pictures and Filmstrips, U.S. Library of Congress, Washington, D.C., 1953-.

53. Check under the various headings in the library catalog where material you need might be found, looking under the most likely headings first.
    a. Follow up clues found in your reading.
    b. Look up cross references.

54. Consult with the librarian or with the director of your study concerning additional guides to material in the field.
    a. Use the *National Union Catalog* to trace books that are not available in your library. This catalog gives information about the libraries which have copies of hard-to-find books.
    b. Check with your librarian to see whether unusual books may be obtained through Interlibrary Loan Service. Books can sometimes be borrowed for limited periods at a cost which usually includes only transportation and insurance.

55. Select sources carefully to be sure you have covered all important phases of the study and the most reliable material on each phase of the study.

56. Read first for an overview—then read more important references critically.

Humbray
The Use . . .
pp. 172-173

Teacher prep.

" ....

p. 173   ..../................"

57. Read critically all the references you find that are related to your study in purpose, method, or findings.

Taking Notes

58. Take all notes on cards of the same size, but use one color of cards for bibliographic data and another (preferably white) for notes on content. (Ordinarily, 3" × 5" cards are the most convenient, but 4" × 6" or 5" × 8" cards may be used.)
59. Record each source and each note on a separate card.
60. If lengthy notes are to be taken, as in the case of copying old records, historical manuscripts, etc., some time-saving mechanical form of duplicating can be used. Such notes would ordinarily be made on 8½" × 11" paper.
61. Be consistent in the form used in taking notes. Use one form on all cards that give bibliographic data and another form on cards on which the content notes are taken.

Notes on bibliography cards

62. At the left-hand margin of the cards that give the bibliographic data, list the following, in the order given:

    Author's full name, with the last name first.

    Full title of the book (or title of the article, if it is a part of a book or if it is an article in a periodical, followed by the title of the book or periodical).

    Series or volume number, if needed (and inclusive page numbers if a part of a book or if an article in a periodical).

    Name of the publisher, place of publication, and date of copyright.

    Total number of pages in a book, unless only a part of the book is referred to.

    Number of volumes, if needed.

63. In the right-hand corner of the bibliography card give the call number of the reference and, just below it, the name of the library where the book was found (unless only one library was used).
64. At the bottom of the card include critical notes about the content, originality, value, conclusions, etc. which you think will help you later in calling to mind the kind of information given in the study and the reactions you had to the book. Use such comments as "very detailed analysis," "contains historical facts," and "of no value."
65. To avoid reviewing the same reference twice, keep the bibliographic card of every reference reviewed, even if the reference is found to be of no value to you.
66. Alphabetize the bibliography cards by author.

Notes on note-taking cards

67. On the note-taking cards, take careful notes on specific facts, ideas, and procedures and on pertinent statements bearing on the problem.
68. On the card on which the notes are taken, list the following:

    a. In the upper left-hand corner write the last name of the author. If references by more than one author by that name have been included, follow the last name by the initials.

    b. If more than one reference by the same author has been used, give an identifying abbreviation of the title just below the author's name.

    c. Below this, place the exact page number on which the quotation appears. If it appears on more than one page, give the inclusive page numbers, marking with a diagonal line the place where the quotation starts on another page and indicating that page number in the left-hand margin.

    d. In the upper right-hand corner tell in an identifying word or two the subject with which the reference deals. Be consistent in the terms or abbreviations used for this purpose. The use of more or less standardized terms for this purpose is helpful.

69. In taking notes, quote the material accurately and put it in quotation marks, to avoid misinterpretations later.
70. Use ellipses (three spaced dots plus the needed punctuation) to indicate omissions in quotations.
71. Place "sic" in brackets immediately after a quoted error to indicate that the error appears in the original. If the quotation is used in the final report, include the word "sic" there also.
72. If you wish to insert your own words in the quotation, place them in brackets (not parentheses).
73. If an entry requires more than one card, number the cards, repeating the author's name on each, and clip the cards together.
74. Check the accuracy of your copying of each reference before going on to the next.

75. Collect more rather than fewer notes than you need. Collect material until references become very repetitious.
76. Note, also, any ideas that come to mind as you go along concerning the development of your study or suggestions for further research.
77. Complete your note-taking in one book before going on to the next.

Filing notes

78. Keep the two kinds of cards in separate boxes and use guide cards.
79. Arrange the cards containing the notes under headings like the identifying terms written on the cards.
80. Make the system flexible so that, if more than one identifying word is used, the cards can be rearranged according to each code word.

Gathering and Checking Data Obtained from Others

Research in general

81. Review the plan so as to have it clearly in mind.
82. Before starting to collect the data know how you are going to process it.
83. Besides using research already completed and published in the field, seek to obtain information from other sources.
    a. Interview persons acquainted with the field and get suggestions from them.
    b. Explain your study to others. This will often clarify your thinking, bring fallacies to your attention, and point out new relationships or approaches.
84. Carry blank cards with you at all times and jot down the suggestions of others as you discuss your study with them. Do not let an idea be lost because you trusted your memory.
85. Develop temporary hypotheses to guide you in carrying on the study.
86. Determine what data are needed to test the hypotheses.
87. Decide on the type of subjects to be used, and check their availability. Be sure to use appropriate subjects.
88. Determine the size of the sample needed.
    a. Make it sufficiently large to be representative of the total population, yet small enough to be handled in the time and with the equipment available. (If a pilot study has been made, statistical techniques may be used on the data obtained to determine the minimum sample size.)
    b. Decide upon the sampling design to use. Two of the most common designs are (1) random sampling, in which names in a population or in a certain strata of a population are drawn by lottery, so that each unit in the population has an equal chance of being included; and (2) sampling by matching, in which units in a defined population are selected which match other units on the basis of certain characteristics. (If an experimental design is used, random assignment is required. If a quasi-experimental design is used, intact groups, such as classrooms, may be used and physical or statistical matching procedures may be appropriate.)
    c. Unless subjects are randomly assigned, the use of volunteers or of only those persons from whom data can be obtained conveniently is likely to bias the findings.
89. Decide on the kind and amount of data needed.
90. Check the data for both internal validity (to see whether they measure what they attempt to measure within the limits of the study) and external validity (to see whether they are applicable to populations similar to those sampled in the study).
91. Check the methods and procedures to be used in securing the data. Use methods that will insure the validity and reliability of the data.
92. Determine the degree of precision needed. Some kinds of studies require much more exact data than others do.
93. Decide on the tools that would be most useful for gathering the data. Use standardized materials and equipment, if possible.
94. If the persons from whom you are seeking information are under someone's supervision, such as employees in a business or children in a school system, seek permission to use these subjects and to obtain the information they can give you.
    a. Understand your problem thoroughly before asking permission to use certain subjects or materials, so as to be prepared to answer questions authorities may ask concerning the study.
    b. Follow proper channels of authority, in seeking permission, asking those of highest authority first.
    c. Explain the study to them, and tell them what you hope to find out and how you think it will benefit them.
95. Never borrow data, material, or equipment without asking permission of those in charge of them.

96. Inquire as to the time that is most convenient for obtaining the information or for borrowing the materials desired, and arrange your schedule accordingly.
97. Use standard data-gathering instruments if applicable, otherwise modify them to meet your needs. If it is necessary to use instruments of your own, be sure they are accurate, reliable, and valid.
98. If possible do not vary the administrator, the interviewer, the observer, or the instrument.
99. Be sure the administrator, interviewer, or observer is qualified and carefully trained for the work.
100. Record data accurately, using standard methods and terms. Give operational definitions for the terms used.
101. Be accurate and consistent in the terms used.
102. Avoid including irrelevant factors.
103. Understand statistics before undertaking a research study requiring statistics.
104. Avoid using unnecessarily elaborate statistical procedure.
105. Set up definite scoring procedures. Keep a careful record of how unusual situations are handled.
106. Try out the study with a small group before starting the study itself.
107. If you are using only a few cases, put the data for each on a hand data card, and keep the data in the same order on all cards. If there are many cases, put the information on data-processing cards to be processed mechanically.
108. If you plan to use data-processing machines in handling your data, be sure you gather your data in such a way that they can be readily handled by the machine in providing the kind of information you are seeking. Inquire as to the form in which questionnaires, tests, etc. should be set up for ease in scoring and tabulating responses.

Historical research

109. If you are making a historical study, one which deals with what events, trends, attitudes, etc. were in the past, seek material that has not previously been unearthed, or relate past events, trends, attitudes, etc. in a way that has not been attempted before.
110. Use only primary sources if possible.
    a. Seek information from biographies; official and historical documents, reports, and records; remains; statutes and court decisions; eyewitness accounts of events; etc.
    b. Use more than one source for each fact.
111. Check the author, to find out whether he is a competent and dependable authority.
112. In collecting material for historical research, check the sources with one another and within themselves for consistency in important facts. Contradictory sources are undependable.
    a. Note the frequency of mention of certain facts.
    b. Watch for bias, propaganda, or misinterpretation of facts.
    c. Check for accuracy, reliability, and purpose.
113. If you are writing a philosophical study, which is subjective, handle it in much the same way as historical research but base it on logic rather than facts. Use critical, objective thinking to discover principles and laws.

Descriptive research

114. If you are writing a descriptive study, attempt not only to gather data concerning existing phenomena, practices, or institutions but also to interpret and evaluate the data in order to establish a norm for the development of these phenomena, practices, or institutions.
115. Decide whether to study a certain situation as it progresses through the years or to study more than one situation in the same stage of development.
116. Select suitable tools and devices for gathering the data (see items 9 to 12). More than one tool may be used.
117. Use any one or a combination of methods of obtaining data.
118. Gather data according to a definite plan.
119. Validate the data-gathering techniques.
120. In a survey type of study, determine existing conditions or relationships between events with the idea of evaluating and improving them, not merely of tabulating them and accepting them. To be considered more than a status study a survey must result in the development or improvement of standards. It is usually used to study and improve a practical situation of local significance.
121. If developing your own rating scale, follow established procedures.
122. Obtain the data in one or more than one way—by questionnaire, rating scale, etc.
123. Check the reliability of the data.
124. Analyze the development and status of an individual, group, or institution.
125. In case studies, which are used especially in social work and are similar to surveys but are usually

based on a much smaller number of cases, use any or several of the tools mentioned for securing information.

    a. Use a prescribed schedule for making observations.

    b. Provide sufficient time for gathering the data.

126. Seek information from the family, friends, school and medical records, employers, physician, psychiatrist, teachers, etc., and visit the home.

127. Collect data that will help you determine the causes of problems and conditions.

128. Apply remedial or adjustment measures.

Experimental research

129. If you are carrying on an experimental study, one in which you base your study on known circumstances and conditions and attempt to learn more facts concerning them and their future, select a simple rather than a complex problem—one which is feasible and solvable.

130. Attempt to discover the effect of a given element.

131. Plan the experiment carefully before undertaking it.

    a. Present the plan so clearly and in such detail that it can be repeated and verified.

    b. Clearly identify and operationally define the dependent variable (the one that is being observed to see whether changes occur in it when exposed to changes in the independent variable) and the independent variable (the one that is manipulated under highly controlled conditions and observed to see whether it affects the dependent variable).

    c. Provide a situation (subjects, procedures, measuring instruments, etc.) in which a single variable can be isolated and varied, and the results can be determined when other variables are held constant.

    d. Point out any variables that are left uncontrolled and explain why.

    e. Use a procedure that does not affect the conditions of the experiment. For example, the response to a brusk examiner might be very different from the response to a congenial one.

    f. Use accurate, scientific instruments and techniques recognized as appropriate for the purpose for which you are using them. Be sure they are discriminating.

    g. Use sufficient time to secure maximum effect.

132. Record each fact and each step in the procedure accurately, giving the time, conditions, controls, etc.

133. In a multifactor experiment, clear your procedure and analysis with an expert in the field before starting the study. Know what statistical design to use and exactly how your data fit into this design.

Using and Developing Data-Gathering Tools

Writing letters requesting information

134. When writing letters to secure information, to control conditions for an experiment, or to request permission to use certain persons, materials, or equipment in gathering or handling data, write a clear, courteous, and businesslike letter.

    a. Type the letter neatly on 8½" x 11" white paper, center it on the page, and single space it unless it is very short.

    b. State the letter in such a way as to create interest in the study and to instill in the recipient a desire to cooperate.

    c. Explain the need for the permission or information requested, and the use to which the information will be put.

    d. If it is possible to obtain official sanction, get the person in authority to sign the letter.

    e. Offer to supply a summary of the results of the study if requested.

135. If a response is expected, be sure to enclose a stamped, self-addressed envelope sufficiently large to accommodate any answer requested or any material to be sent to you and give the final date when responses should be received.

136. If you promise to keep in confidence the information sent to you, be sure to do so.

137. If possible, address the letter to the person who would give the permission or information rather than merely to the position.

138. Always put the return address on both the letter and the envelope.

Preparing pencil-and-paper instruments

139. If information is to be obtained by having the subjects fill out a pencil-and-paper instrument, select a standard instrument of recognized worth that is appropriate for use in the kind of study you are

undertaking and for the purpose for which you are using it.

140. If no suitable standard instrument is available, prepare your own, but check it for appropriateness, completeness, understandability, reliability, and validity before using it in the final study.

141. In preparing a pencil-and-paper instrument in which the information sought is to be filled in by others (such as a check list, questionnaire, inventory, or opinionnaire), consider (a) the plan and purpose of the study, (b) the kind of people from whom information is being requested, (c) the kinds of information needed, and (d) the ways in which the returns are to be handled.

142. Remember that the returns on instruments to be answered in writing by others may be biased by the fact that some who are asked to check the instrument do not respond and that some respond in the way in which they think you want them to respond. To check the bias of your returns compare the respondents with the nonrespondents on demographic data.

143. Request only relevant information (a) that is of importance to the study, (b) that the respondents can furnish or secure easily, and (c) that they are qualified to provide and will provide willingly.

144. Have the instrument printed, multilithed, or mimeographed on paper that will take ink.
    a. Make the instrument attractive in appearance, neat and well balanced on the page, and compact.
    b. If, in reproducing the instrument, it is reduced in size, be sure to keep the type large enough to be easily read.
    c. Leave sufficient space for the respondents to answer the questions in the blanks provided.
    d. See that the finished instrument is a size that can be sent in a standard size envelope and can be easily handled and filed.
    e. Have a sufficient number of copies made to provide for follow-up and for file copies to be sent if requested.
    f. Duplicate on thesis paper the copies to be included in the final report.

Developing questionnaires and opinionnaires

145. Use a questionnaire or opinionnaire only when the information needed can be obtained in no other way, since the results may so easily be biased by carelessly made responses, omission of responses, or willfully made incorrect responses.

146. Use a questionnaire to gather factual information rather than opinions, unless the opinions are sought from those who are particularly qualified to answer.

   a. In using "closed" questions, list all the possible answers. For example, in classifying a certain book, if the choices concerning the grades for which it is suitable are "the lower elementary grades," "the intermediate grades," and "neither," the respondent may be forced to answer inaccurately as his correct response may be "both lower elementary and intermediate grades" or "don't know." Thus, five rather than three choices should be given as possible responses if this is to be a closed question.
   b. In "open" questions, invite free response at the end of a list of specific items. For example, in listing types of clubs, include "civic," "cultural," "recreational," "religious," "social," and "other," since you cannot cover all possible answers. This type of question makes it possible to learn of the respondent's motives and attitudes. Remember, however, that free response items are difficult to tabulate and summarize.

147. Use an opinionnaire when seeking opinions or attitudes. The findings of the opinionnaire are more difficult to report than those of the questionnaire because the responses are more subjective. (In assessing attitudes one of the well-known techniques for developing scales should be used as a guide.)

148. At the top of the instrument, provide blanks for the respondent to give his name, position, and address (unless the instrument is to be filled out anonymously).

149. Structure the questionnaire carefully, to get as complete and honest a response as possible.

150. Make the general directions and the directions for each part clear and explicit.
    a. In the general directions, give an estimate of the time required for answering.
    b. Define any terms used that may be misunderstood or that have a special meaning in the study.

151. Arrange the questions in some kind of logical order. Group those seeking the same kind of information, putting the simpler and more direct questions first in each section.

152. Include only questions dealing with specific aspects of your objectives or hypotheses.

153. State the questions simply and so clearly that the answers can mean only one thing.
    a. Avoid two-in-one questions. For example, "How many employees were absent because of sickness or death in the family?" It may later be found important to know how many were absent for only one of these reasons.
    b. Avoid questions whose answers may not be comparable. For example, in the question above, un-

less "in the family" is clarified, some respondents may include the employee himself and some may not. Or, in questions such as one concerning the annual salaries of teachers, the responses may not be comparable unless the number of months of teaching in a year is known.

    c. Avoid ambiguous questions. For example, "Rate the following from 1 to 5" does not indicate whether the lowest or the highest is to be given the rating of 5.

    d. Avoid leading questions. For example, "Do you agree with the rules set up by those who have studied the problem?"

    e. Avoid incomplete questions. Are you married? Yes__ No__ How about widowed and divorced?

154. State the questions so that they can be answered quickly, easily, and objectively—by a check, a number, or only a word or two.

155. If possible, state the questions in all parts of the instrument so that the answers can be given in a uniform style.

156. To facilitate the tabulation of the data, place all the blanks for responses either immediately preceding the number of the question immediately following it, or at the right-hand margin.

157. If the responses are to be punched on IBM cards for quick rearrangement and tabulation by machine, code the questions. Get information from the person who will be responsible for punching the cards to be sure the items are set up and coded in such a way as to make this mechanically possible.

158. When the instrument is believed to be complete, check it for repetitions, contradictions, and inconsistencies.

159. Have a competent research person check the instrument when you feel it is ready for use; then revise it, if necessary, in the light of the suggestions he may make.

160. Try out the instrument in a pretest with a small representative group.

    a. Check the results of the pretest to determine the instrument's completeness, clarity of instructions and questions, and appropriateness for gathering and manipulating the data, etc. before starting to collect the data for the study.

    b. Make any revisions in the instrument that are necessary before undertaking the gathering of data for the research.

161. At the end of the instrument give the name, position, and address of the person to whom it is to be returned.

Using standardized tests and other measuring devices

162. If you need an objective measuring device, select a recognized standardized test, rating scale, or scorecard in the field.

163. Become well acquainted with the measuring device you plan to use, and with the instructions for giving and scoring it, before attempting to use it.

164. If no standardized measure is available that fills your purposes, prepare one of your own.

165. Make the instrument meet the following qualifications:

    a. Make it valid (measure what it claims to measure).

    b. Make it reliable (measure accurately and consistently).

    c. Make it objective (free of bias or personal judgment).

    d. Make it sufficiently detailed to give exact information.

    e. Keep it within the comprehension of those on the educational level for which it is designed.

    f. Make it economical (in both time and money).

    g. Plan it so that it will be easy to administer and score.

166. Develop a key, with specific directions for scoring.

167. If it is necessary to have more than one person administer the device, select persons with suitable preparation and experience and give them explicit directions and training.

Seeking information through interviews

168. If you seek information through interviews, use a guide prepared in advance and worded carefully in order to keep the interview on the subject and to obtain the information you are seeking.

169. See the rules for the questionnaire. The interview is an oral questionnaire in which the ability to read is not important and an opportunity is given for exchange of ideas.

170. Be well informed in the area in which information is sought.

171. Prepare the questions in advance, wording them carefully, in order that information of the same type may be obtained from each person interviewed.

172. Have a standard way of recording the answers to questions.

173. If possible, tape record the pilot study so that results can be studied carefully and the questions can be revised if necessary.

174. Interview only people who are qualified to answer questions on the subject.

175. Make arrangements with the interviewee ahead of time.
    a. Ask him for his permission to hold the interview, and explain the purpose of the study and the need for the information.
    b. Arrange a definite time for the interview, at his convenience.
    c. Make an effort to gain his confidence and respect.
176. Do not spend any more time than is necessary with each person.
177. Be well informed in the field of study, so that you can modify your tactics if necessary when interviewing a subject.
178. Avoid leading questions. (See item 153d.)
179. Adapt the interview procedure to the type of person whom you are interviewing.
180. Take advantage of the opportunity to reword any questions which the interviewee needs clarified and to probe deeper if this will throw more light on the problem.
181. Follow up the responses, pick up and develop leads, and attempt to bring out the reasons for certain responses.
182. If possible, tape record the interview so that it can be played back and studied. This will speed the interview, reduce the amount of note-taking, and result in more accurate interpretation of the responses.
183. Avoid asking personal or confidential questions. When such information is sought, assure the interviewee that you will not disclose his identity —and keep your word.

Seeking information through observation

184. When seeking data through observation, use a guide similar to that used for the interview, listing the points for which you are looking, in order to objectify your observations. This can be set up in the form of a rating scale or check list, but care must be taken not to make it too detailed.
185. Seek only pertinent data that you can obtain objectively, and have a clear-cut idea of what you want to observe.
    a. Do not attempt to collect more data than you can handle in the time available, or to collect the kind that cannot be easily recognized.
    b. Be able to evaluate and describe, both quickly and accurately, the factors observed.
186. Avoid using very complicated activities or activities that are not easily recognized.
187. Do as little writing as possible, but do not depend on memory.
188. If possible, use a one-way screen when observing, so that those being observed will not be influenced by the presence of the observer; if not possible, accustom the persons to the presence of observers before collecting the data for the study, so that the findings will be based on a normal situation.
189. If available, use cameras, tape recorders, etc. that make a permanent record of the occurrence. Recordings can be played back and photographs can be studied later.

Handling the Data

Research in general

190. Study the data carefully and set forth the steps to be taken in handling them.
191. Classify the data by categories that are appropriate, clearly defined, and of a type that will bring out significant relationships, likenesses, and differences.
    a. Classify them in an orderly and logical manner; i.e., according to topic, date, geographical location, etc.
    b. Classify them according to one factor at a time, first in terms of the larger differences and then in terms of lesser differences.
    c. Present the data as clearly as possible.
192. Inspect the data thoughtfully and carefully when they are classified, noting the relationships of various factors and the recurring sequences and trends.

193. If data are collected by means of questionnaires, tests, etc., store these in a safe place, so that they can be referred to if any questions arise later concerning the data.
194. Decide upon the techniques to be used in analyzing the data and justify their use. Use methods that will insure the validity and reliability of the data.
195. In studies in which it is necessary to make decisions in classifying or analyzing certain cases, keep a record of the decisions made in order that your interpretation of data may be consistent.
196. Use recognized standard measures and instruments. If none are available, construct some that will meet your needs. Check the reliability and validity of these.
197. In analyzing the data, use the techniques or skills that will best carry out the plan of the study and that will not affect the conditions of the study.

a. Use specified standards for analyzing the data.

b. Analyze the data for meaning and draw inferences. Do not overanalyze.

c. Use vision in analyzing the data, but base the analysis on reasoning.

198. Use machine tabulating and scoring whenever available, not only to save time and worry with routine work but also to insure greater accuracy. Check the material for accuracy in punching cards and in machine as well as hand scoring.

199. Check all manipulations of the data to be sure they are logical and accurate.

200. Before attempting to analyze the data statistically, be sure you know statistical procedures and how to use them in research.

a. Be sure that the type of statistics used fits the data you have collected and the purpose for which the statistics are used.

b. Use standardized statistical terms in presenting the analysis of the data unless the data are unusual.

201. Do not use complicated statistical techniques on relatively simple data.

202. Do not expect complicated statistical techniques to improve faulty raw data.

203. If mechanical means of handling the data are not available, use tables of reciprocals and square roots to save time and to reduce the chance of inaccuracies in computation.

204. Study the results carefully to see whether the study has made a contribution.

a. Relate the data to the conditions and needs of the situation being investigated.

b. Be accurate and logical in the interpretation of the data. Acknowledge the limitations of the study.

205. When comparing elements, use a uniform basis for comparison. Do not describe some in terms of fractions, some in terms of percentage, and some in terms of ratios. Percentages are the most accurate; fractions and ratios are very effective in showing relationships.

206. Be objective and open-minded in interpreting the findings.

a. Interpret the findings accurately.

b. Do not base reasoning on lack of facts, faulty analogy, or silence.

c. Do not bias the results of the study by omitting some of the subjects, returns, or data.

207. Evaluate the findings according to recognized standards. Eliminate those that are not relevant to the study. (Check with the hypothesis.) Subordinate those that are not the principal findings.

208. Do not overgeneralize. Usually the findings will be limited by the degree to which they have external validity.

209. Use originality and judgment in interpreting the findings but keep a scientific viewpoint.

210. Seek an explanation for the findings.

Historical research

211. In historical research, organize and interpret significant past facts and trends in attitudes or events.

a. Select and reject facts carefully.

b. Show their relationship to one another and their contribution to present-day practices and understandings.

212. Use footnotes especially in this kind of research, as the authenticity of the resources is extremely important.

213. Do not interpret old documents in the light of the present.

214. Do not assume that all items in a source are true when some are true.

Descriptive research

215. In handling the data in descriptive research, give a detailed account of the steps taken in gathering the data.

216. Study a situation over a period of time or study several situations in the same phase of development at one time.

217. Do not try to match the cases on too many variables.

218. To avoid losing too many cases in matching, use an appropriate statistical matching technique, such as analysis of covariance.

219. In interpreting the findings, do not assume that present practices are correct.

a. Evaluate them.

b. Watch for flaws in your reasoning.

c. Be objective and discriminating.

220. On the basis of the interpretation of the findings, establish a norm.

Experimental research

221. In conducting an experiment, control the factors involved so that any change effected by them will be small enough to be unimportant.

222. Manipulate the independent variables under highly controlled conditions.

223. Explain how the variables are manipulated.

224. Describe the equipment and controls for each step.

225. Check carefully, on the basis of standard measures, the effect on the dependent variable resulting, presumably, from exposure to the independent variable. Be alert to any changes that take place.

226. Keep an exact and complete record of what takes place, recording each fact and the details of each step in the procedure, and giving the time, conditions, controls, etc.

227. In true experimental research with random assignment of subjects, measure the dependent variable at the end of each treatment; in quasi-experimental studies measure it at both the beginning and the end of each step.

228. Isolate various factors and conditions to determine whether they have affected the results.

229. Present the experiment so clearly and in such detail that it can be repeated and verified.

230. Seek an explanation of the findings.

231. Look for cause and effect relationships and determine why a particular condition exists.

232. Generalize and formulate theories and principles. (Experimental studies are usually more generalizable than quasi-experimental studies.)

233. Verify the generalizations by repeating the experiment or by using additional data in another experiment.

234. Use tables and figures only to clarify, support, or illustrate the findings or to point out relationships and similarities.
    a. Keep tables and figures as concise and simple as possible.
    b. Show not more than two or three kinds of closely related facts in a single table or figure.
    c. Make tables and figures sufficiently informative that they can be correctly interpreted without reference to the text.

235. Explain in the text the generalizations derived from the table. Point out such things as trends, unusual findings, etc.

THE WRITING OF THE RESEARCH REPORT

Outlining the Final Study

236. Outline the final report, revising the outline as additional material is found and new ideas come to mind.

237. Organize the study logically, so that the reader can easily follow the progress of facts and ideas. Set up the outline in such a way that the relationship of the topics to one another is clear.

238. Avoid overlapping between main headings and subheadings under them.

239. Do not divide the study into a great many chapters, divisions, and subdivisions.

240. Number the chapter titles in Arabic numerals and make them and other headings meaningful. Do not call them merely "Introduction," "Findings," and "Conclusions."

241. Make all headings on the same level of equal importance and consistent in terminology and grammatical form.

242. In this outline state each topic in sentence form, so that a person reading the outline can get a general idea of the content as well as of the organization of study.

243. In the introduction to the study, present the problem and its background.

244. In the body of the study, report all the information needed for a full understanding of the performance and findings of the study.
    a. Include a detailed account of the sources of data.
    b. Discuss in detail the methods and procedure used.
    c. Present a critical analysis and evaluation of the data.
    d. Present and interpret the findings.

245. Make each division complete, including tables, etc., before going on to the next division.

246. Eliminate superfluous material.

247. Do not include material in the body of the study that should be in the appendix.

248. In the concluding chapter, summarize the study, draw conclusions from the findings, and present the recommendations (if included).

Writing the First Draft

Providing good working conditions

249. Work willingly and persistently.

250. When writing, avoid interruptions or competing interests that break into your periods of work and disturb your trend of thought. On the other hand, do not work too steadily. Get completely away from the problem now and then to free your thinking.

251. Do not work when you are tired or worried about other things; i.e., when you cannot give your whole attention to the study.

252. Keep handy at all times a dictionary, a thesaurus, and the reference books and files you are using.

253. Leave wide margins on the typed copy, so that there is plenty of room for insertions and corrections.

254. Budget your time.
    a. Set up time limits for each phase of the study and try to meet them.
    b. Plan your work so that you can be writing one part while you are temporarily delayed on another. For example, work on the review of literature or some other part of the study while waiting for data to be gathered or tabulated or for the director of your study to go over and criticize a section you have completed.

255. Make a carbon copy of the rough draft and of each revision as insurance in case anything happens to the original. Do not keep these with the original. Put the date on each copy and revision so that you will know which is the most recent.

Thinking through the problem

256. Give the study a meaningful and concise title. Do not introduce it with "A Study of" or "An Investigation of."

257. Before starting to write the first draft, review your notes carefully to refresh your mind concerning their content and organization. (Take all the notes you expect to take before starting to write, but do not hesitate to add others later.)

258. Read the outline through carefully to get a picture of the study in its entirety.

259. Contemplate on the problem until your mind is saturated with it and continue to think through the study as the writing progresses. This will build a trend of thought that will lead to new ideas.

260. Sort out the reference cards that deal with the point on which you are working.
    a. Read and organize them carefully before beginning to write that part.
    b. When you have used a reference cross it out on the card to avoid using it a second time.

261. Since your thinking must be clear before your writing can be clear, be sure you understand the problem and the meaning of the data you have collected before you begin to write.

262. Do not add personal comment.

263. Be impersonal. Write in third person. Avoid editorial "we," "the present writer," etc. For example, say "personal letters were sent to all subjects," not "the writer sent personal letters to all subjects."

264. In writing the first draft, do not spend undue time on style. Concentrate on putting your ideas on paper. Then polish the report and improve the mechanics later.

265. Complete the discussion in each division before going on to the next.

Writing the introduction

266. Show enthusiasm for your study.
    a. Tell how you happened to select the topic.
    b. Explain why you think the study is needed, how it will extend knowledge in the field, and in what other ways you think the findings will be of value.

267. Present the problem fully and accurately, and point out the limitations of the study.

268. Explain the subject before giving the historical background.

269. In the historical background of the study, include only significant material that is needed to orient the reader.

270. Set up hypotheses that are objective, that are consistent with the facts, and that provide a framework for the study.

271. State the hypotheses clearly, preferably in the form of null hypotheses, so that they can be tested statistically to find whether any differences are significant or whether they are merely a matter of chance. Present the assumptions on which they are based.

272. Eliminate any temporary hypotheses set up that you have been unable to defend.

273. Describe briefly the sources of data, the types of data used, the materials and equipment needed, and

the methods and procedures used in analyzing the data (but seldom those tried and discarded).

274. Define all unusual terms used.

   a. Include all technical terms used.

   b. Include all other terms used with a specific and slightly different meaning from the usual.

   c. Place the terms in quotation marks the first time they are used, defining them at that time; then treat them like any other words in the study after they have been defined.

Writing the review of related research

275. Check through the studies you have read and include a review of only those references that make a contribution to your study in purpose, method, materials and tools used, or conclusions. If this review is long, it should probably be a separate chapter.

   a. Make clear the relationship of these studies to your own study.

   b. Organize the references by date, purpose, similarity of population, geographical area, or some other plan.

   c. If several pages of references are reviewed, summarize them by groups if they are divided into groups, or as a whole at the end of the section if they are not.

276. If previous studies in the field are lacking, relate the study to the philosphy underlying the problem.

Quoting from other studies

277. If you plan to include quotations from other studies in the final report, include them in the first draft of the study.

   a. Quote from other references only when the original cannot be said as clearly or accurately in any other way or when there is some other good reason for preserving the wording. Rarely is it necessary to quote a long passage.

   b. Do not lift or use quoted material in such a way as to distort the meaning.

   c. If only a sentence fragment is being quoted, make it fit into your sentence both grammatically and coherently. If it is introduced in the middle of a sentence thought, do not capitalize the first word, even though it may be capitalized in the original.

   d. Be accurate in every detail, including in the original any errors found and indicating the places where you have omitted parts of the quotation. (See items 70 and 71.)

   e. Do not use ellipses either at the beginning or at the end of a quotation unless they are needed for clarity. Word the introduction to the quotation and the text following it so that the thought flows smoothly, without need for the omitted material.

278. Single space all quotations of four or more lines, indenting them three spaces from either side and leaving a triple space both above and below them.

279. Double space between paragraphs of single-spaced material.

280. When quoting from different authors with no intervening comment, set the quotations a triple space apart.

281. Obtain written permission to use anything quoted from copyrighted material, regardless of its length. This is both an ethical and a legal obligation.

   a. Write to the holder of the copyright for permission to quote. This is usually the publisher (sometimes the author) of printed material; the author, producer, or sponsor of radio or television programs; or the producer or owner of the negative of motion pictures, filmstrips, recordings, or transcriptions.

   b. Submit any unpublished material you are quoting, such as lectures or personal letters, to the person being quoted for his approval and permission to quote.

282. When paraphrasing, do not include anything that is not in the original; on the other hand, omit nothing of importance.

   a. Be original in the way you paraphrase, thus keeping a unity of tone and personal style in your study.

   b. Do not merely change a word or two and consider it as paraphrasing.

Including footnotes

283. Use footnotes to acknowledge the source of ideas or material borrowed, to establish authority for a statement that may be challenged, to refer to related materials elsewhere in the study, or to avoid interrupting the thought in the text by including a detailed explanation or elaboration of some point.

   a. Include in the first draft all footnotes that will be needed in the final revision of the study.

   b. Include a footnote for each quotation and for each paraphrased idea, giving the source of the material.

   c. Do not ordinarily include footnote references to proverbs and familiar quotations or to classics which appear in many different editions. In the case of the latter, however, if it seems advisable to give the page number, also include the name of the book and publisher and the edition used.

284. Be consistent in the form for footnotes used to acknowledge the source of a statement. In references to books, give the author's last name, followed by his initials, the title of the book, and the pages on which the reference is found (or the total number of pages in the book if the whole book is referred to).

In references to parts of books, follow the form used in the bibliography (see item 325d), except that the initials should be used and the publication data should not be included.

In references to articles in periodicals, follow the form used in the bibliography (see item 325e), except that the author's initials and the exact pages referred to should be used.

285. If a publisher specifies the footnote form to be used when he grants permission to quote a passage, use that form even though it may not be consistent with the form used in the other footnotes.

286. Number all footnotes in the content in the same numbering system. Use Arabic numerals, and number the footnotes consecutively, beginning with *1* in each chapter.

287. Indicate footnotes to tables, diagrams, maps, or other illustrative materials or to data included in them, by symbols rather than by numbers.
    a. Place the footnotes immediately after the illustration rather than at the bottom of the page and keep them within the margins of the illustration.
    b. Use the following symbols: *, *, *, #, **, **, **, ##, in the order given.
    c. Begin the notes on each separate table or figure with the asterisk (*).

288. Place the footnote number immediately after the quotation and either after the borrowed idea or after the author's name in paraphrased or borrowed material (but be consistent in the plan used).

289. When a numbered bibliography instead of footnotes to references is the style adopted, place the number of the reference in parentheses after the borrowed material.
    a. If a page number is needed for the reference, separate it from the reference number by a colon.
    b. Use symbols like those used in tables to designate footnotes other than references to published material (see item 287), and use them consecutively within each chapter.

290. Avoid cross references in the text, especially those to references in later sections of the report, because of the difficulty of having them inserted in the final typed copy.

Writing the body of the report

291. In writing the body of the report, seek to discover the interrelationships among the various types of data obtained and reflect on their meaning.

292. If previous studies in the field are lacking, relate the study to the philosophy underlying the problem.

293. Try to give the reader a more informative interpretation of the topic than he can find elsewhere. (Include everything you think might help develop the study, as it is easier to eliminate than to add material later.)

294. Describe the data clearly and accurately, telling in detail how, when, and where the data were collected and how they were analyzed and classified.

295. Present the data and the procedures used in such detail that others can repeat the study and verify the findings.
    a. Do not merely present the data, interpret them.
    b. Do not spend time stating accepted facts, like "the data were carefully tabulated to avoid errors."
    c. Explain the methods of procedure, setting forth the steps taken and moving logically from one step to the next.

296. Describe in detail new apparatus or instruments used, or variations of old ones, and explain their use.

297. If statistical procedures are used in handling the data, include the formulas used only when they are unusual or original. Standard statistical procedure should be identified but need not be explained in detail.

298. Present the data from different points of view. Point out similarities, irregularities, trends, etc.

299. Evaluate the findings and interpret them in the light of the purposes of the study. If they do not agree with accepted opinion, tell how and why.

300. If interesting findings are discovered other than those expected, point them out.

301. Point out the possible errors, the gaps in data or thought, or the findings that are contrary to the findings of others, and explain the reasons for these.

302. Do not accept or state as fact either your own opinions or those of other individuals or groups unless you can support your statements with data, with examples of other studies which substantiate them, or with reports by recognized authorities.

303. Be ready to defend your interpretations. If someone disagrees with a statement you cannot defend, admit the fact that you cannot defend it.

304. Make the discussion of each division complete before going on to the next division.

Including illustrative materials

305. Include in the first draft all illustrative material you plan to use in the final study.

306. Avoid using too many tables, examples, quotations, etc. Include only those that add to the meaning and clarity of the study.

307. Present the data in tabular or graphic form, if feasible, when it will be helpful to the reader. (For correct form for tables and figures, see Dugdale, Kathleen, *A Manual of Form for Theses and Term Reports,* which is listed in the Bibliography, page 45.)

308. If tables are included in the study, number them consecutively throughout the study (including the appendix) and use the number in referring to them. Do this also for figures (including charts, diagrams, maps, and photographs in the same series).

309. Introduce each table or figure before inserting it.

310. Make table and figure titles concise and clear enough to be correctly interpreted without reference to the text.

   a. Make them consistent within the series in both terminology and grammatical form.

   b. Do not begin a title with such expressions as "A Table Showing," "A Map of," or "An Illustration of."

   c. Place table titles in capital letters at the top of the table.

   d. Place figure titles below the figure, with only the first letters of principal words capitalized.

311. If any ink work is needed on a table or figure, use black ink, as the colors cannot be duplicated or microfilmed.

312. See that all tables and figures are well constructed and that they point up significant relationships.

313. Discuss each table and figure after it has been inserted, pointing out the significant facts, trends, etc. Do not merely repeat the information given in the table or figure.

314. When statistics are discussed that are not shown in the text, inform the reader of this.

Writing the concluding chapter

315. Make the last chapter clear and concise, since it is the most often read.

316. Although the concluding chapter ordinarily includes the summary, conclusions, and recommendations, do not include all three unless they are appropriate for the type of study you have written.

Summary

317. In the summary, give a comprehensive integrated report of the study.

   a. Restate the problem, including a brief general view of the sources and nature of the data and the methods and procedures used.

   b. Simplify the problem so that those who have not read the whole study will know what it concerns.

   c. Do not include anything in the summary that has not been discussed in the earlier part of the report.

   d. Present the findings in the order in which they have been presented in the body of the report.

   e. Emphasize the significant aspects of the study, but do not rehash the details.

   f. Point out the contribution of the study and the implications of the findings.

318. If the findings have modified existing theory, explain in what way they have done so.

Conclusions

319. In drawing conclusions, suspend judgment until all the facts are before you and you have given them careful thought.

   a. Be sure the conclusions are pertinent to the objectives of the study and are justified by the data, that they are either positively or negatively constructive, and that they are complete so far as the data indicate.

   b. Be objective. Point out the limitations of the data, partly proved conclusions, etc. Do not ignore adverse evidence.

   c. Avoid including any preconceived ideas.

   d. Do not overstate the conclusions. In most cases the findings are true only for the population on which they are based.

320. Present the conclusions in the same order as the findings on which they are based.

321. Check to be sure you have answered all of the questions and tested all of the hypotheses set forth in the introductory chapter.

Recommendations

322. Make clear but brief recommendations, based on the data and findings of the study.

   a. Consider in the recommendations the phases of the study which need further investigation, the possible applications of the facts and theories

brought to light in the study, and the related problems worthy of investigation.
  - b. Consider the difficulties involved in fulfilling the recommendations.
  - c. Justify the recommendations in the light of the possible objections and prejudices of those who will appraise them.
323. If certain implications (well organized thoughts and concepts) have developed out of the study, include these also.

Making up the supplementary pages

Bibliography

324. Make the bibliography selective rather than all-inclusive.
  - a. Include all references you have read and used in the study and all you have referred to in the footnotes, but list none that you have not examined.
  - b. Do not include personal letters, diaries, etc. that are not available to the public, or materials that have proved to be of no value to your study.
325. Set the references up in the following form: (See Dugdale, Kathleen, *A Manual of Form for Theses and Term Reports,* listed on p. 45.)
  - a. Include all the references in the same list.
  - b. Include in each book reference the author's full name (with the last name first), the name of the publication (underscored), the publisher, the place of publication, the copyright date, and the total number of pages, in that order. Separate these items by commas. For example, Bernstein, Theodore M., *Watch Your Language,* Pocket Books, Inc., New York, 1965, 213 pp.
  - c. Set up each bulletin reference like a book reference, inserting the bulletin series and number after the title. For example, Lynch, William W., *Instructional Objectives and the Mentally Retarded Child,* Bulletin of the School of Education, vol. 43, no. 2, Indiana University, Bloomington, March, 1967, 54 pp.
  - d. Include in each reference to a chapter or article in a book or bulletin the author's full name (with the last name first), the title of the chapter or article (in quotation marks), the word "in" followed by the title of the book or bulletin (underscored), the inclusive page numbers on which the chapter or article appears, and the rest of the publication data listed for books or bulletins, except that the total number of pages should be omitted. For example, Moore, O. K., and Anderson, A. R., "The Structure of Personality," in *Motivation and Social Interaction,* pp. 167-186, edited by O. J. Harvey, The Ronald Press Co., New York, 1963.
  - e. Include in each reference to an article in a periodical the author's full name (with the last name first), the title of the article (in quotation marks), the name of the magazine (underscored) followed without punctuation by the volume number (in Arabic numerals), a colon, the inclusive page numbers, and the date (month, day if necessary, and year). For example, Maciuszko, George, "Polish Education in Exile," *School and Society* 79: 134-135, May 1, 1954.
326. Alphabetize the references according to the author's last name, or according to the title if no one is named as responsible for the study.
  - a. Alphabetize as separate words compound proper names that are not hyphenated; alphabetize as one word those that are hyphenated.
  - b. Alphabetize names with such prefixes as "de," "le," and "von" by the prefix if it is part of the specific last name, and by the first letter of the last name if it is not. (Ordinarily the prefix is considered a part of the last name if it is capitalized.)
  - c. Alphabetize names beginning with "M'," "Mc," and "Mac" as if they were one word beginning with "mac."
  - d. Alphabetize names beginning with "St." as if the word "Saint" were written out.

Appendix

327. Include in the appendix all material needed as evidence for the content that is too detailed, too cumbersome, too formal, or too mechanical to be included in the study itself without interrupting the sequence of thought. Include only supporting material that is important and justified, such as letters (but not those requesting information unless there is some special reason to do so), questionnaires, raw data, explanation of a data-gathering instrument or a detailed computational technique devised for the study, excerpts from documents, diaries, or legal papers, etc.

Index

328. An index is seldom needed in a thesis, but if it is included, make it sufficiently detailed to be readily usable, but do not include useless entries.
  - a. Use key words, preferably in noun form, that are familiar to the reader.
  - b. Alphabetize all items in the same list.
  - c. Include cross references when necessary, but use them sparingly.

Revising the Report

329. Allow plenty of time for revision.

330. Do not start to revise the report until all material is in and the writing of the first draft is completed.

331. Set the written report of the research aside for at least 24 hours (preferably for several days) in order to get a better perspective before starting on each revision.

332. Then reread the report, checking one type of revision at a time. Do this carefully, as the weaknesses in the completed study will be quickly recognized by those who matter.

333. Reconsider the title in light of the completed study to see whether it is concise yet descriptive of the study.

334. Take particular care to check the organization of the study.
    a. Check to see that the study is developed logically.
    b. See that each stage leads further toward the completion of the study.
    c. See that the relationship of the different parts of the study is evident and that the parts are given the proper emphasis.
    d. Check for consistency in purpose and point of view.

335. Check for content.
    a. Clarify places that do not seem clear.
    b. Check to see that no gaps are left in the thought.
    c. Check for repetition of facts or ideas.
    d. Search for flaws in reasoning.

336. Admit and discuss any weaknesses you find that you cannot correct.

337. Be sure that all necessary material is included, and that unnecessary or irrelevant material is not. Expand points when desirable; eliminate those that add nothing.

338. Check for consistency in style of writing.

339. Check for correctness in rhetorical form and grammar.
    a. Rearrange paragraphs, or chapters if necessary, for the better organization of material.
    b. Check transitions to be sure they are smooth after the material is rearranged.
    c. Clarify statements or discussions where needed.

340. Check for consistency in spelling, capitalization, and punctuation.

341. Check for accuracy in data, computations, quotations, bibliographic data, etc.

342. Type a list of chapter, division, and subdivision headings.
    a. Check each to see that it is worded so as to relate that section to the thought of the study as a whole.
    b. See that the terminology and grammatical form of headings on the same level is consistent.
    c. Check table headings and figure headings in the same way.

343. Do not number or letter division or subdivision headings.

344. When rearranging copy, cut and paste (with rubber cement preferably) rather than retype large amounts of material. Avoid using a transparent tape like Scotch tape on the typed side of the paper (some kinds of which will take neither ink nor lead) or staples (which catch and make the material hard to handle).

345. Retype often-revised and corrected material rather than try to work with copy that is hard to read and to follow.

346. Seek honest constructive criticism from an editor, if possible, who will go over the manuscript after you have done your best without his help.

347. If possible, have someone read the manuscript aloud to you. This will bring out lack of clarity and of consistency more quickly than if you, who are acquainted with the study, should read it.

348. Put corrections in the margins or between lines.

349. After all corrections and changes have been made, type the final copy.
    a. Use a style manual, as you cannot be consistent in form unless you have rules to follow. (See Dugdale, Kathleen, *A Manual of Form for Theses and Term Reports*, which is listed in the Bibliography, page 45.)
    b. Remember that both the content and the form of the final report are very important, as a poorly presented study reflects on both the author and the university.

350. Proofread the final copy carefully, checking especially for accuracy.

351. Save all carbon copies and all notes at least until the final thesis is accepted and in the library.

352. When the study is completed, send a summary to those to whom you have promised to send summaries. (See item 134e.)

SUGGESTIONS FOR CLEAR AND EFFECTIVE WRITING
Making the Report Rhetorically Correct

353. Write so that the average interested person can understand the report. Do not assume that the reader has the knowledge of the subject that you have.

354. Present the material logically and fluently. Good writing is never easy, but it should appear to be easy, i.e., it should be so clear and well organized that the train of thought can be followed readily and accurately, with no concern for the mechanics of the report.

355. Make the writing alive. Convey a sense of fact, letting the worth of the study make it interesting.

356. Construct your sentences and paragraphs in such a way that your report has unity, coherence, emphasis, and clarity.

   a. Give the study unity, or singleness of purpose and thought, by keeping a definite goal and a consistent and logical point of view.

   b. Give the study coherence by making the thought flow smoothly from one thought to the next. Arrange words, sentences, paragraphs, sections, and chapters so that they logically follow what has immediately preceded.

   c. Place the emphasis on the more important ideas by giving them more space than the less important ones; by placing them in the first or last position in the sentence, paragraph, or division; by using appropriate connectives, punctuation, etc.; or by arranging them in order of climax.

   d. Secure clarity by using comparatively simple vocabulary and sentence structure and by writing in a straight-forward way, making each thought grow out of the last or relating it to the study in such a way that the reader has no difficulty in understanding its relative importance.

357. In the introduction of each chapter, describe the part of the study to be discussed in that chapter. At the end, include a paragraph or two of generalization of the material included in the chapter.

358. Do not destroy the continuity of thought by calling attention to the structure of the study. For example, a chapter should begin with a transition statement such as "After the data had been secured and the returns were divided according to the age, education, and experience of the employees," rather than with "In Chapter II the returns will be divided and discussed under the following three headings: age, education, and experience." If a study is well organized, this fact will be recognized by the logical flow of ideas without the structure being pointed out to the reader.

359. Increase interest by making a point important to the continuity in almost every paragraph, thus keeping the study moving toward accomplishing its purpose.

360. Make the first sentence in each chapter or division complete within itself, not dependent on the heading for its meaning. For example, after a heading like "The Problem of Water Supply," do not begin the first sentence with a statement like "This problem was a serious one." State the problem, even though it has already been stated in the heading.

361. Treat each topic as a separate unit and complete the discussion of that topic before going on to the next.

362. Include only one idea or one phase of an idea in a paragraph, but include all the facts necessary for a full understanding of that point.

363. In each paragraph have a topic sentence that states the central idea being developed.

364. Place the topic sentence anywhere in the paragraph, but phrase it so that there is no doubt about its being the central thought of the paragraph. For example, "The most evident change necessary involved the hiring of more highly trained workers."

365. Present the ideas in a natural, orderly sequence, making each sentence contribute to the central thought.

366. Avoid unnecessary and unimportant detail, too many qualifications of incidental points, and needless repetition of an idea.

367. Word the last sentence of each paragraph in such a way that it gives the impression of completeness and points ahead to the idea presented in the next paragraph. For example, "These facts led to but one conclusion—that changes would have to be made if the business was to grow."

368. In the last paragraph of each chapter, give the impression of completeness and of a well-rounded

whole. Never have a weak or abrupt ending to a chapter.

369. Use transitional sentences to carry the meaning from one paragraph to the next, introducing them with "flashback" expressions like "as has been suggested," "if this is true," "the second factor," and "as a result." Do not overdo the use of such expressions.

370. Keep the introductory, transitional, and concluding paragraphs short.

371. Use the concluding paragraphs to summarize, condense, and recapitulate.

Making the Report Grammatically Correct

Using good sentence structure

372. Do not write sentences merely so that they can be understood—write them so that they cannot be misunderstood. Use good organization, good connectives, and correct grammar.

373. Let your sentence structure be determined by the relationship of the ideas to be expressed. They will then almost always follow grammatical rules.

374. Strive for simplicity, clarity, and directness. Be logical and consistent.

375. State sentences in such a way as to show their relationship to one another.

376. Avoid having too many small units set off by commas, as this causes jerky rhythm. For example, "They reported, as they had been requested to do, that, although it was late, they would try, if at all possible, to get to the meeting on time."

377. Give emphasis by using short pithy sentences, but avoid too many short sentences.

378. Be sure a sentence containing a parenthetical expression would be grammatically correct if the parenthetical expression were omitted.

379. Gain variety in your sentences by varying the length and grammatical organization of the sentences, varying the beginnings of the sentences, inverting the order of the main elements and of phrases and other modifiers, using apositives, etc.

380. Avoid using more words, phrases, and clauses than necessary to make the meaning clear. Simplify wordy expressions like the following. For example, say "In the group, 45 percent were men," not "In the group 45 percent were men and 55 percent were women." Or say, "They plan to visit additional schools in 1962," not "They have completed plans to continue the visitations of an additional number of schools in the year 1962." Or say, "The closing hymn," not "The hymn that was sung at the close of the service."

381. Avoid beginning a sentence with "there is" or "it is." For example, say "Three said . . .," not "There were three who said . . ." Or say, "Seven of the eight items listed on the questionnaire were checked," not "There were eight items listed on the questionnaire and seven of them were checked."

382. Do not make remarks like "it is interesting to note" unless you can prove it is interesting.

383. Do not omit words needed for clarity; that is, say "I understand that the difficulty caused by his arrest arose from . . ." not "I understand the difficulty caused by his arrest arose from . . ."

384. Do not place "that" in a sentence both before and after an intervening phrase or clause. The position of "that" in the sentence depends upon the meaning to be conveyed. For example, say "He said, when he came, that he would call us." or "He said that, when he came, he would call us." Not "He said that, when he came, that he would call us."

385. If desired for emphasis or as a continuation or summing up, begin a sentence with "and," "for," "or," etc., but do not overdo this. For example, "And at last they reached the peak," "But the sense of unreality frightened them."

386. Emphasize an idea by repeating a prominent word or phrase. For example, "He was soaking wet—his clothes were wet, his hair was wet, and even the package he carried was wet."

387. Place words and phrases so that there will be no question as to the exact meaning to be conveyed by the sentence.
   a. Place words like "only" and "even" near the words they modify (usually just before the words they modify). In the following sentences, note the differences in meaning:
   "Only his assistant can sign that check."
   "His only assistant can sign that check."
   "His assistant can only sign that check."
   "His assistant can sign only that check."
   b. Place negatives immediately before the word they modify. In the following sentences, note the changes in meaning:
   "Not all the trains were late."
   "All the trains were not late."
   "Everything not in print is founded on fact."
   "Everything in print is not founded on fact."
   "Not everything in print is founded on fact."

c. Avoid placing modifiers where they may give the sentence a double meaning. For example, "They have looked forward to visiting us for a long time."

388. When a positive and a negative idea appear in the same sentence, ordinarily express the positive idea first. For example, say "The goal should be desired practice rather than existing practice," not "The goal should not be existing but desired practice."

389. Place the adverb between the auxiliary and the rest of the verb when used with a compound verb, and between the auxiliary and the complement when used with a copulative verb. For example, "I have already won," "It is often true."

Using parallel constructions

390. For effectiveness, use grammatically parallel movement and balanced sentences to contrast or show likenesses between ideas in parts of a sentence or between whole sentences that are logically parallel.

    a. Include in the second part of a parallel construction all the words necessary to make the construction complete. For example, say "She wore clothes that were better than those of the other girls," not "She wore clothes that were better than the other girls."

    b. Repeat prepositions and conjunctions in parallel constructions and place them immediately before the parallel terms. For example, "He peeped in not only through the door but also through the window," "He went not only for my sake but for his own satisfaction."

Listing items in series

391. Do not list unrelated items in the same series, or qualify one or two of the items in such a way that the qualification seems to apply to all the items in the series. For example, say "Reports were made of the lighting and ventilation and of the appearance of the teacher," not "Reports were made of the lighting, ventilation, and appearance of the teacher."

392. When giving a series of items do not include the article or the introductory preposition with any but the first item unless you include it with every item or phrase in the series. For example, say "The box contained a brush, towel, and rubber sponge," not "The box contained a brush, towel, and a rubber sponge."

393. If some of the items in a series are modified by the article "a" and some by the article "an," the article should be repeated with each item. For example, "an orange, a pear, an apple, and a peach."

394. Do not use "etc." at the end of a series of words or phrases introduced by "like" or "such as."

395. When items are listed by name in a series, alphabetize them unless some characteristic such as date or size is more important.

Placing prepositions at the end of a sentence

396. Avoid ending a sentence with a preposition. Say "The person with whom we stayed," not "The person we stayed with."

    a. If it is awkward to place the prepositional phrase earlier in the sentence, put the preposition at the end. For example, "He knew what it was meant for."

    b. If the preposition is needed to complete the meaning of the verb, put it at the end. For example, "They listened to the conversation we were carrying on."

Stating comparisons clearly

397. In comparisons, liken the thing being explained to something already familiar to the reader.

398. In a series of discussions or comparisons of the characteristics of two or more groups of people, things, or ideas, mention the same one first in each comparison, and present them all in the same grammatical form.

399. When comparing one person or thing with the rest of its class, use such a word as "other" or "else" with the comparative. For example, "He was taller than any other boy (not "than all the boys") on the team."

400. Avoid the awkwardness of using two kinds of comparison in the same sentence. Complete one comparison before beginning another. Say "Helen is at least as tall as my sister," not "Helen is as tall as or taller than my sister."

401. To avoid ambiguity in comparisons, repeat the verb after "than." "Mary likes me better than you do," not "Mary likes me better than you."

402. Avoid unfinished comparisons, such as "He went further this time." "They are most interesting."

403. Use the comparative when comparing two things. "Of the two plans this is the less (not "least") effective."

404. Do not compare words that are not comparable, such as "full," "impossible," "unique," and "square."

405. Use "more" and "most" when comparing words of three syllables or more; "-er" and "-est" when comparing words of one syllable; and either when comparing words of two syllables.

Using pronouns properly

406. Make the pronoun agree with its antecedent in number and person and put it in the case required by its position in the sentence. For example, "The girl who is coming," "The girls whom we knew."

407. Do not attempt to clarify a statement like "John told Allen that he (John) made a B on the test" by inserting the antecedent in parentheses. Rewrite the statement.

408. Never place a pronoun before the word for which it stands (except in the few cases in which it is done for emphasis). For example, say "The items listed were screws, nuts, and bolts," not "The list contained these items: screws, nuts, and bolts"; "This we knew: that they had arrived on Friday."

409. Place modifiers so that their antecedents will be clear. Otherwise the thought in the sentence may be ambiguous, and even in some cases ridiculous. For example, "He took the gifts from the boxes and left them on the floor," "I saw an eagle flying through my binoculars."

410. Do not use a pronoun to refer to a word in the possessive case. "The house belongs to John who owns the market," not "The house is John's, who owns the market."

411. Do not use a pronoun to refer to a word in a dependent or unemphatic position. "The remark was made to a boy in the group who came late."

412. Avoid reference to a general idea or to a vague or implied antecedent. For example, say "Oranges are grown in Florida," not "In Florida they grow oranges"; "Being so close to being elected and then losing the election was a disappointment," not "Being so close to being elected and then losing it was a disappointment."

Using possessives correctly

413. Use the form of the possessive pronoun that is correct for the position where it occurs in the sentence. Say, "It is for her as well as his benefit," not "It is for hers as well as his benefit."

414. Do not use a possessive to express the object of an action. Say "The rescue of the child," not "The child's rescue."

415. Do not use the possessive for inanimate objects except in the case of time. For example, say "the dog's bone," "a three weeks' trip," but not "the house's roof." Expressions concerning time and weight can be made into compound adjectives, like "a five-day vacation."

Using correct verb forms

416. For clarity's sake, have a subject and a verb in each sentence. Avoid such expressions as "So much for that" and "Hence the problem about dates." Phrases may stand as sentences in literary works but are not desirable in research.

Number

417. Always make the verb agree with the subject, regardless of the number of the predicate complement, the addition of phrases and clauses, etc. For example, "Bananas are one kind of fruit he can eat." "One kind of fruit he can eat is bananas." "This, together with the facts cited, makes it necessary to deny the request."

418. In the case of collective nouns used as the subject, use a singular verb if they are thought of as a group and a plural verb if they are thought of as individuals acting independently. For example, "The rest of the paper was thrown away." "The rest of the papers were scattered throughout the area." "More than 50 per cent of the group is made up of farmers," "More than 50 per cent of the group are active members in their own churches."

419. Use a singular verb in the following cases:
When "many a" is the subject, even when followed by a compound subject. For example, "Many a soldier and sailor has entered the service as a career."
When the subject is "more than one." For example, "More than one accident has taken place at that crossing."
When the subject is singular in meaning but plural in form. For example, "Measles is sometimes serious." "Ten miles is too far to walk."

420. In a compound sentence, do not omit the verb in the second clause when one clause is singular and the other is plural. Say, "The moon was bright and the stars were clear," not "The moon was bright and the stars clear."

421. When the same verb is used in both clauses in a compound sentence, do not omit the stem of the verb in the second clause unless it is in the same form as that in the first clause. Say, "I work hard and always have worked hard," not "I work hard and always have."

422. Use a singular verb with firm names or literary titles. For example, "Harper and Row is the publisher," "*Tales of a Wayside Inn* is on the required reading list."

423. When a sum of money or a measure is the subject, use a singular verb if it is thought of as an amount, a plural if it is thought of as independent units. For example, "Five dollars is all I need," "Three quarts are in pint containers."

424. When a compound subject is made up of two singular nouns joined by "and," use a plural verb unless the two are so closely associated in one's mind that they would be considered as one. For example, "Bread and butter are among the items on the grocery list," "Bread and butter comes with the meal."

425. If one part of a compound subject is affirmative and one is negative, the verb should agree with the affirmative. For example, "He, not I, is invited," "I, not he, am invited."

426. If the parts of a compound subject are joined by "or," "nor," or some such expression as "not only . . . but also," the verb should agree with the subject nearest it. For example, "He or they have to stay home," "They or he has to stay home."

Tense

427. Be consistent in the tense used, to avoid uncertainty concerning the time relationship of the statements made.
   a. In reporting research, usually use the past tense for presenting the purposes, reviewing the literature, describing the methods, and presenting the findings. Data, while accurate when collected, may no longer be truly representative when the study is being written.
   b. Use the present tense when presenting general conclusions and when stating other facts that are believed to be universally or permanently true. This is true even when the general truths are stated in a clause which is subordinate to one in the past tense. For example, "He contended that tomatoes are classed as fruits."
   c. Use the perfect tense forms to express action that has been completed at some time earlier than the action in a related clause. For example, "They were working when their father arrived, but they had been (not "were") playing before that."

Voice

428. As a rule, use the active voice rather than the passive, as it is stronger in effect, more direct in meaning, and simpler in statement.
   a. Avoid needless shifts in voice, for, while this may vary the style, it changes the point of view and often clouds the meaning. For example, say "They returned before they received the word," not "They returned before the word was received."
   b. Use the passive voice when the "doer" is either not known or not to be disclosed. For example, "The package had been opened."
   c. Avoid double passives, as in "The report was expected to be completed by Friday."

Mood

429. Use the indicative mood in statements believed to be true. For example, "If Bert is here, he is here for a purpose."

430. Use the subjunctive mood only when necessary.
   a. Use the subjunctive when you wish to imply that you do not believe that the statement you are making is correct. For example, "If that be the case, the problem is simple."
   b. Use the subjunctive after verbs of resolving, ordering, suggesting, recommending, and so forth and after statements of necessity when followed by a clause introduced by "that." For example, "They demanded that he be asked to resign," "I move that the secretary write a note of thanks."
   c. If several recommendations or suggestions are listed in the study, set them up as independent statements (using the auxiliary "should" with the indicative form of the verb) rather than introduce each by "that" (using the subjunctive and having the recommendations depend on the introductory statement for their full meaning). For example, "The following recommendations are made: (1) The building should be moved; (2) . . ." not "It is recommended: (1) that the building be moved; (2) that . . ."

Infinitives, participles, and gerunds

431. Be sure the infinitive, participle, or gerund placed at the beginning of a sentence refers to the subject of the principal verb. For example, say "To see well, you should have stronger glasses," not "To see well, your glasses should be stronger"; "When Formula 3 was used, the r was found to be .47," not "By using Formula 3, the r was found to be .47."

432. Do not "split" an infinitive (that is, put a modifier between "to" and the verb) except when it is necessary to avoid awkwardness or misinterpretation, as in "He hoped to more fully meet necessary expenses for his college education."; "He was asked to state his reasons clearly," not "He was asked to clearly state his reasons."
   a. Repeat the "to" with each verb in a series of infinitives if other qualifying words intervene. For example, "He was expected to prepare a speech that evening and to deliver it next morning."
   b. Use an infinitive rather than a verbal noun. "My job was to collect," not "The collection of."

433. Be sure a participle within or at the end of a sentence refers to the nearest noun or pronoun preceding it (unless you are expressing general rather than specific action by the participle). For example, "Crossing the lake, they caught three fish," not "They caught three fish crossing the lake"; "Generally speaking, few accidents were reported by the police."

434. Use the possessive case rather than the objective of nouns and pronouns used with a gerund. For example, "He was interested in the boy's swimming." Otherwise the gerund becomes the verb in an understood clause and the meaning of the sentence is changed. For example, "He was interested in the boy (who was) swimming."

Selecting Appropriate Vocabulary

435. Use simple, dignified words that are appropriate to research writing, are within the comprehension of the audience for whom you are writing, and are as interesting as is consistent with scientific accuracy.

    a. Avoid the use of intensives. For example, "They were very good (not *so good*) to me.

    b. Use words like "reported" and "indicated" rather than "felt" and "thought" when discussing the data in a study.

    c. Do not express an idea in a foreign language when there is an English equivalent. For example, say "coffee," not "café."

    d. Avoid provincialisms. For example, use "intelligent," not "smart"; "repair," not "fix."

    e. Avoid trite expressions. For example, "abreast of the times," and "breathless silence."

    f. Avoid tautology. For example, "free gratis," "old adage," "wise sage."

    g. Avoid poetic terms such as "ere" and "amidst."

    h. Avoid unnecessary prefixes and suffixes, such as "ornamentation" for "ornaments."

    i. Use the terms "male" and "female" only when referring to sex, not when referring to people. Say "All 40 men and 50 women," not "All 40 males and 50 females."

436. Do not overwork certain terms, like "however," "thus," and "in other words."

437. Do not try to vary vocabulary if it destroys clarity. For example, do not refer to the subjects as "students," "pupils," "boys and girls," "young men and women" at different times, as the reader then has to check to be sure you are referring to the same group.

438. Watch the sound of sentences. Read the material aloud.

    a. Avoid alliteration (except for effect), rhyme, and repetition.

    b. Avoid having several words in a sentence that sound harsh together. For example, "hopelessly helpless," "decidedly gregarious," "stated statistically."

439. Use accurate qualifying words that contribute to the exact meaning.

    a. Use abstract words to express ideas, generalizations, etc., such as "honesty," "virtue," "dissatisfaction."

    b. Use specific, concrete words with established meaning to give an exact meaning, such as "robin" for "bird."

    c. Use words with pleasant connotations, such as "inexpensive" for "cheap," and "slender" for "thin."

    d. Use action words that give energy, clarity, and beauty, such as "bounded," "specified," "radiated."

    e. Avoid weak qualifying words like "rather typical."

440. When looking up a word for synonyms be careful to select the synonym in a thesaurus or dictionary that best expresses the meaning you are trying to convey. Not all synonyms are appropriate in all places. For example, in choosing a synonym for "smell," use "aroma" when describing a strong, pleasant smell (such as cigars); "fragrance" when describing flowers; "scent" when telling about perfumes; and "odor" when describing a strong, perhaps unpleasant, smell (such as gas).

441. Use figures of speech sparingly in a research report. If you use them, word them correctly. Do not mix them with literal expressions or with other figures of speech.

442. Do not use shortened forms of words. For example, say "gymnasium," "telephone," and "photograph," not "gym," "phone," and "photo."

443. Avoid repetition of words except for emphasis.

444. Avoid using a word in two senses in the same sentence. For example do not say "They planned to have the plan ready by Friday."

445. Omit titles like "Dean," "Professor," "Dr.," and "Mr." except in the acknowledgment.

Using Correct Spelling and Capitalization

446. In order to be consistent throughout the study, make a style sheet of the spellings, hyphenations, and capitalizations used.

447. Consult the dictionary if there is any question concerning the spelling of a word or its compounds. (If more than one spelling is acceptable, the one given first in the dictionary is the preferred form.)

448. Do not use the accent marks on foreign words which have become Anglicized unless they are necessary

to clarify the pronunciation. For example, "regime," "résumé."

449. Do not add "ed" to form the past tense of most verbs ending in "cast." For example, "broadcast," "forecast."

450. Use the English spelling of names of foreign cities or other geographical areas. For example, "Bern," "Naples."

Forming plurals

451. Use the American plural of foreign terms, except when the foreign plural is in general use. For example, "curriculums," "data."

452. Add *es* to form the plural of proper names ending in *s* or *z*. Add *s* to those ending in *y*. For example, "Rexes," "Lewises," "Fays."

453. Add an apostrophe and *s* to form the plural of words except when they have an established plural. For example, "if's and and's," "yeses and noes."

454. Add an apostrophe and *s* to form the plural of dates, numbers, single letters, signs, abbreviations made up of initials, etc. For example, "Ph.D.'s," "r's," "1960's," "3's."

455. Add *s* at the end of the final syllable to form the plural of nouns ending in "ful." For example, "teaspoonfuls."

456. In compound words, form the plural by adding an *s* to the principal word. For example, brothers-in-law," "adjutant generals," "passersby." If there is no principal word, pluralize the last word. For example, "also-rans," "take-offs."

Forming possessives

457. Add an apostrophe and *s* to form the possessive of singular words ending in *s*, *x*, and *z*, but add only the apostrophe to form the possessive of plural words ending in *s*. For example, "the fox's tail," "the witness' testimony," "the animals' actions."

458. Add the apostrophe or the apostrophe and *s* to only the last name in the case of joint possession, but to each name if each owns a thing separately. For example, "Dick's and Harry's coats," "Johnson and Wright's book."

459. Use an "of" phrase rather than the possessive of long names. Say "The action of the Society for the Prevention of Cruelty to Animals," not "The Society for the Prevention of Cruelty to Animals' action."

460. Add the apostrophe or the apostrophe and *s* to the last word of compound terms to form the possessive, like "somebody else's opinion."

461. Do not use the possessive where words are more descriptive than possessive, as in "teachers meeting" and "United States laws," except in the case of "men" and "women" in terms like "women's club."

Hyphenating

462. Use a hyphen when necessary for clarity to combine words into an adjective phrase which precedes the word that is modified. For example, "six-foot soldiers," "six foot-soldiers."

463. Use a hyphen to prevent misunderstanding, mispronunciation, or awkward spelling. For example, "re-cover," "co-author," "semi-invalid."

464. Use a hyphen in a modifier that consists of an adjective or adverb and a word ending in "ed" unless the first word in the modifier is a comparative or an adverb ending in "ly." For example "a high-priced book," "a higher priced book," "a highly developed technique."

465. Use a hyphen to join elements of an improvised word. For example, "make-believe," "know-how," "pay-as-you-go."

466. Unless awkward spelling results, write as one word, without a hyphen, often-used combinations of an active verb and a preposition. For example, "layoff," "setup."

467. Do not hyphenate rather long combinations of words that would be clear without the hyphen. For example, "teacher training institution," "cancer experiment station."

468. Do not ordinarily hyphenate compounds of the prefix "non" except when used with proper nouns or when needed for clarity. For example, "nonexistent," "non-Catholic."

469. Words ending in "fold," "hand," or "wise," should not usually be hyphenated. For example, "fourfold," "firsthand," "crosswise."

470. When the common element in a series of hyphenated adjectives is omitted in all except one item in the series, use a hyphen with each item, with a space between it and the next word in all except the last item of the series. For example, "one-, two-, and three-story houses."

471. Hyphenate expressions like "out-of-date" and "out-of-town" when used as adjectives.

Abbreviating

472. In the body of the report, avoid using any but customary abbreviations, such as "Mr.," "i.e.," and "a.m."

473. If it is necessary to use a less well known abbreviation, use the one that is established through usage.

If none is established, write out the word or words the first time they are used, placing the abbreviation in parentheses immediately after them, or in a footnote. Thereafter, use the abbreviation.

474. Follow each abbreviation by a period except in the following cases:

When a letter is used as a substitute for a noun rather than as an initial. For example, "Mr. X went to town."

When an agency, organization, broadcasting station, etc. is perhaps better known by its initials than by its full name, such as "UNESCO," "YMCA," "NBC."

Expressing numbers

475. Be consistent in using either figures or words to express numbers. A desirable way is to write out whole numbers below 10 (except identifying numbers like "grade 6") and to use figures for numbers of 10 and above.

476. In ratios or in lists or comparisons of amounts, all numbers should be given in figures if any of them are 10 or above.

477. When referring to decades, write out the years if only the decade is given, but use figures if the century is also given. For example, "the late forties," "the late 1940's."

Capitalizing correctly

478. Use no more capital letters than necessary.

479. Capitalize the first letters of principal words (all words except articles, conjunctions, and prepositions of four letters or less) in titles of publications, in filmstrips, motion pictures, tests, recordings, etc., or in major parts of these.

480. Capitalize the following:

Titles of specific courses in school. For example, "Introduction to Research."

Major parts of a manuscript followed by identifying numbers or letters, but not minor parts. For example, "Act I," "Table 3," "Chapter 4," "page 5," "footnote 24."

The first word of every item when the items are set up in the form of a list.

The first word in a statement that follows a colon, provided it is a complete sentence.

Prepositions that are a part of a verb, like "carry out" when the verb is capitalized.

The second half of a capitalized hyphenated word.

481. Do not capitalize the following:

Names of subject areas or of class standing in school. For example, "mathematics," "sophomores."

Names of seasons.

The words "federal government" and the word "state" in expressions like "the state of Colorado."

Generic terms when used in the plural. For example, "Fifth and Sixth streets."

The name of a position or governing body when used as a general term. For example, "the superintendent of schools."

The terms "ex," "elect," etc. in titles. For example, "Governor-elect," "ex-President."

Using Correct Punctuation

482. Since the purpose of punctuation is to make the meaning of a sentence clear and effective, keep uppermost in mind the thought that you wish to convey when deciding on the punctuation to be used. Good judgment in this respect is often as important as rules in showing the proper relationship of the ideas presented.

483. Be sure you know the various purposes for which the different punctuation marks can be used. On the whole, only those uses are included here which it is thought the research writer might need to look up.

Brackets

484. Within direct quotations use brackets around the word "sic," around an editorial explanation or insertion, or around a correction. For example, "They arrested two boys [not the two being sought] who were acting suspiciously."

485. Use brackets to set off interpolated material, such as stage directions or editorial explanations. For example, "Mr. Adams [entering at left]: Sorry to be late."

486. Use brackets to enclose parenthetical material which contains material in parentheses.

Colon

487. Use a colon to separate two main clauses when the second explains or illustrates the first. For example, "The train passes through town twice a day: it is north-bound in the morning and southbound in the evening."

488. Use a colon following a complete statement that introduces an enumeration, a long quotation, a question, or a summarizing clause,

provided the statement before the colon is grammatically complete. For example, "The following persons were present: Mr. and Mrs. Brown, Mary Smith,...." not "The persons present were: Mr. and Mrs. Brown, Mary Smith,...."

489. Use a colon to separate the title of a book from the subtitle.

490. Use a colon to follow the name of a speaker in a play or in a recorded conversation.

Comma

491. Use commas in the following places:

Between all items in a series of words, phrases, or clauses set off by numbers or letters in parentheses, unless the items are in sentence form or are long and involved.

Between items that would not be clear if not separated. For example, "Soon after, I went to Chicago," "All who spoke, spoke well."

Between simple, independent clauses joined by a coordinating conjunction, provided the subject changes. For example, "They worked hard but took regular vacations," "They worked hard, but John took his vacation."

To set off non-restrictive (but not restrictive) words, phrases, or clauses. For example, "A boy, lonely and frightened, hid in the dark," "The research covering the period 1825 to 1875 was analyzed."

To separate related consecutive word groups introduced by "not" and "but." For example, "He ran away, not because he was unhappy but because he wanted to see the world."

Between interdependent clauses. For example, "The slower the machine operated, the easier it was to handle."

To separate coordinate adjectives. For example, "He was very, very sure," "Dr. Black was a cold, unfriendly, unhappy man." If "and" cannot logically be inserted after the last comma, do not separate the adjectives with commas. For example, "Five happy little girls."

To set off interrupting words or phrases, unless the interruption is slight. For example, "You see, therefore, that the job can be completed soon," "You see that the job can therefore be completed soon."

To set off the name of the state when used to identify a city, and the year when used with the month. For example, "He arrived in Springfield, Missouri, in May, 1967."

To indicate the omission of one or more words in expressing a thought. For example, "Being a member is one thing; being an officer, another."

After an introductory word, phrase, or clause unless it is very short, is closely related to the thought, or is not needed to give the full meaning of the statement. For example, "Consequently he could not get there on time," "During the months that followed, many meetings were held."

Before, but not after, words like "such as" and "especially" if a pause is needed, when they are used to introduce explanatory material. For example, "He sold such notions as thread, needles, and pins," "He sold notions, such as thread, needles, and pins."

In all figures of 1,000 or more, except in addresses, dates, decimals, page numbers, and serial numbers.

492. Do not use a comma in the following places:

To set off a quoted statement that is a grammatical part of the sentence. For example, "He read the directive that 'everyone should stay away from the area'."

In compound statements of weight, measure, or time. For example, "14 pounds 10 ounces," "10 years 11 months."

Between a name and the word "of" used to introduce its place or position. For example, "Johnson Dairy of Richmond," "President Stahr of Indiana University."

Before an adverbial clause which completes the thought of the preceding main clause. For example, "He arrived late because his train was delayed."

To separate a verb from its subject, complement, or direct object. Nonrestrictive materials set off by commas may be inserted between the two, however. For example, "Most of the men, and some of the women also, gave at least a little."

Dash

493. Use a dash between a long enumeration at the beginning of a sentence and the summarizing expression. For example, "Corn, rye, barley, and wheat—these are the grains that are grown in the area."

494. Use a dash to indicate an afterthought or a sudden break in thought or sentence structure. For example, "He arrived on time—in fact, an hour early." "The boy—if it was a boy—disappeared around the corner."

Exclamation point

495. Never use the exclamation point to give emphasis in research.

Italics

496. Seldom use italics (which is indicated by underscoring in typewritten material) for emphasis. Rewrite the sentence so that the meaning is clear and the wording and organization of the sentence place the emphasis where it belongs.

497. Use italics for the names of books, periodicals, and other published works; filmstrips, recordings, and motion pictures; and ships, aircraft, trains, paintings, operas, etc.

498. Use italics for foreign words, the word "Resolved" in a resolution, and a single letter or number used as a word. For example, "Your *n*'s and *u*'s look alike."

499. Do not italicize a letter used as a name, like "Mr. C."

500. Do not italicize the name of the Bible or of parts of the Bible.

Leaders

501. Use leaders in the table of contents, to lead the eye to the page number.

502. Use leaders made up of three spaced dots plus punctuation to indicate an omission in a quotation. For example, "He was ready . . . , but he fell asleep."

Parentheses

503. Do not use parentheses if commas will serve the purpose.

504. Use parentheses to enclose explanations or other essential information that is only loosely connected with the text. For example, "One of the other schools (Lincoln) was almost as large as Scott School."

505. Do not precede a parenthetical expression within a sentence by any mark of punctuation other than the first parenthesis, but follow it by whatever punctuation besides the closing parenthesis would be needed in the sentence if the parenthetical expression were omitted. If the entire sentence is enclosed in parentheses, the end punctuation should also be enclosed in parentheses.

506. Except in legal material, do not repeat in parentheses a number that has been spelled out.

507. Use parentheses around letters or numbers designating subdivisions within a sentence. Do not use periods, either inside or outside the parentheses.

508. When referring to references in a numbered bibliography, put the numbers in parentheses.

Period

509. Use a period after the final item of a list when the list as a whole completes a sentence; use it after each item only when the items are in sentence form or when they are in a list of items, part of which require periods.

510. Use a period following numbers or letters used to identify paragraphs or items in lists, unless these numbers or letters are in parentheses.

511. Do not use periods after Roman numerals (except in enumerated lists), after contractions, after shortened forms of names, after sums of money given in even dollars, after the word "percent," or after headings that stand alone.

Question mark

512. When an exact date or term has not been established but is thought to be correct, use a question mark in parentheses immediately following the statement in doubt. For example, "His first novel, written in 1796(?), was based on the political situation."

513. In compound questions, place a question mark only at the end of the sentence unless each item is to be answered independently of the others. For example, "Did he go to England, Scotland, or Wales?" "Did he go to England? Scotland? Wales?"

514. Do not use a question mark after an indirect or a polite question.

Quotation marks

515. Enclose in quotation marks the titles of parts of published works, such as articles in a magazine or chapters in a book; parts of symphonies or operas; and parts of radio and TV programs.

516. Do not use quotation marks around the comments of participants in write-ups of discussions when the participants' names introduce and immediately precede the comments. For example, "Mr. Jones: It is with pleasure that . . ."

517. Use quotation marks to set off words referred to as words. For example, "The concepts 'good' and 'bad'."

518. Do not use quotation marks when expressing your own questions. "The question is: How can this be done?"

519. Do not use quotation marks to set off references to the preface, introduction, bibliography, appendix, or index of a specific work.

520. Do not use quotation marks to enclose inserted quotations of four or more lines. These should be indented and single spaced instead. (See items 278-280.)

521. Use quotation marks around quotations in footnotes, regardless of the length of the quotation.

522. Always place the quotation marks outside periods and commas. Place them inside question marks and exclamation points if the question or exclamation is a part of the sentence; outside, if it is the whole sentence.

523. Use single quotation marks to enclose a quotation within a quotation.

Semicolon

524. Use a semicolon between coordinate clauses that are joined by a conjunction if the clauses are long or if they contain other punctuation. For example, "If he wins, I will go to New York; but if he does not, I will remain here."

525. Separate items in a series by semicolons if they contain commas and are neither numbered nor lettered. For example, "Kent, Connecticut; Dover, Delaware; and Atlanta, Georgia."

526. Use a semicolon before the word that introduces an explanatory or summarizing statement. "He did many things that were frowned upon; for example, . . ."

TROUBLESOME WORDS AND CONSTRUCTIONS

a—should be used before words beginning with a consonant sound. "A history," "a eulogy," "a one-time winner."

an—should be used before words beginning with a vowel sound. "An orange," "an 1890 model," "an *m*."

abide *by* (not *with*) a decision.

ability *to do* (not *of doing*).

ability—mental power plus training. "He has the ability to teach science."

capacity—native mental power. "He has the capacity to memorize quickly."

about—should not be used to mean *almost* or *nearly*. See *approximately,* and *as to*

above (prep.)—in a higher place, in excess of.
Should not be used as an adjective in such expressions as "the above question." "The question above" or "the foregoing question" should be used instead.
Should not be used to refer to content on a previous page.

accent (verb)—to stress. "He accented the last syllable."

accentuate—to draw attention to. "He accentuated his remarks with . . ."

account—should not be followed by *as*. "I account it a piece (not *as a piece*) of good fortune."

accurate—truthful and complete in detail. "His description of the murderer was accurate."

correct—conforming to a standard. "His answers on the test were correct."

acquaint—to make aware of or familiar with. "Acquaint him with the situation."

advise—to counsel or warn. "Advise against his making the trip."

inform—to impart facts. "Inform him of the committee's action."

notify—to inform by notice. "Notify him by air mail."

acquiesce—to comply without opposition, but with reluctance. "He acquiesced to the plan, as it seemed he had no alternative."

acquire—to get possession of by any means. "He acquired a fortune through family ties."

obtain—to get hold of by effort. "He obtained his degree in three years."

A.D.—in the year of our Lord. Can be used only with specific dates and should always be placed before the date.

B.C.—before Christ. Can be used with eras, centuries, etc., as well as with specific dates, and should always be placed after the date.

adapt—to make fit or suitable. "He adapted the plan to his needs."

adopt—to take as one's own. "He adopted the plan used by similar organizations."

addicted to—persistently devoted to. "He is addicted to drugs."

subject to—liable to or dependent on. "His child is subject to colds." "The policy is subject to the approval of the Council."

admission—right of entrance. "Your ticket assures you of admission."

admittance—act of entering. "The ticket-taker gives you admittance when you present a ticket."

admit—to acknowledge as true. "He admitted that he had been at the party."

confess—to admit one's errors or guilt. "He confessed that he stole the money."

adopt—see *adapt*.

advance (noun)—progress. "The advance in educational television."

advancement—promotion. "His advancement to the office of president."

adverse to—to be opposed to. "Adverse to the attorney's report."

averse to—to have distaste for. "Averse to rich food."

adviser—is preferable to *advisor*.

affect (verb)—to influence. "The weather affects his arthritis."

effect (verb)—to bring about or result in something. "Invention of the steam engine effected changes in transportation."

effect (noun)—the influence or result of some action. "The effect was remarkably beautiful."

aforementioned—should be used as a pronoun in legal documents only.

after—unnecessary before a perfect participle when used to introduce a sentence. "(After) having made this known, he left for New York."

again—should not be used with verbs of action beginning with the prefix *re* (meaning *again*) unless it is a second repetition.

ago—a qualifying clause that follows *ago* should begin with *that* (not *since*). "It was more than six years ago that (not *since*) he was in Boston."

agree *in* a characteristic.
agree *on* a plan.
agree *to* a doctrine or proposal.
agree *with* a person.

agree—to be in harmony with. "They agreed with the doctor."

assent—to agree by act of understanding. "They assented to every suggestion."

comply—to agree by yielding to another. "He complied with his father's request."

concur—to agree in opinion. "The group concurred with the chairman."

consent—to agree by act of will. "They consented to take the trip."

aggravate—to make worse or more intense (not *to annoy*).

aggregate (noun)—total in mass (not in sums of money).

aim—that toward which efforts are directed.
end—one's ultimate purpose in the work he is undertaking.
object—the thing one is planning to achieve.

alike—redundant when used with the word *both* in constructions like "We are (both) alike in that respect."

alike—having a sameness in certain definite respects.
identical—having a sameness in all respects.
similar—having a general likeness.
synonymous—alike in word meaning.

all (adj.)—should not be followed by *of* when used with a noun. "List all the names."

all (noun)—should be followed by *of* when used with a pronoun. "List all of them."

allege—to state positively but without proof. "It is alleged that the warden helped the convict escape."

assert—to declare with assurance. "He asserted his rights."

claim—to assert something which should be acknowledged or conceded. "He claimed he had won the contest."

allude to—to refer to something indirectly or lightly. "He alluded to our being late."
refer to—to make mention of a thing specifically. "He referred to Jack's wedding."
allusion—indirect or casual reference to something. "The allusion is to a passage in literature."
delusion—false belief held persistently. "He is under the delusion that he is manager."
illusion—false impression. "He had the illusion that the doorbell rang."

ally—an associate in affairs of state.
colleague—an associate in a professional group.
partner—an associate in a business.

almost (adv.)—quite, very nearly.
most (adv.)—in the highest or greatest degree.

alone—unaccompanied (not *only*).

aloof *from* (not *of* or *to*).

also—when used as a conjunction, *and* should be added. "He drove to Mexico and also to California."
See *another*.

alternative—a choice between two things or courses. Should not be used with *only*. (Redundant) "The alternative was to drive all night."
choice—a selection made from two or more things, on the basis of judgment. "The choice was to be made from among the best-sellers."
preference—a selection made on the basis of desire. "His preference would be to make the trip next week."

although, though—should not be followed by such words as *nevertheless, however,* or *yet*. (Redundant) "Although he knew better, he came late (not *yet he came late*)."
although—should usually be used to introduce a clause that precedes the main clause.
though—should usually be used to introduce a clause that follows the main clause.

alumnus, alumni—masculine singular and plural forms.
alumna, alumnae—feminine singular and plural forms.

America—should not be used for *the United States*.

among, between—should not be followed by *each* or *every* and the singular. "Between scenes (not *between every scene*)."
among—should be used when referring to more than two persons or things. "He divided the seeds among the farmers."
between—should be used when referring to only two persons or things, or to more than two if they are closely related or if only two of them are considered at a time. "The prize was divided between the athlete and his manager." "Correlations between achievement test scores, intelligence test scores, and class grades were high."
Never introduce the second term by *or*. "The choice is between writing and (not *or*) calling by phone."

amount—quantity thought of as a unit. "The amount of food was adequate."
number—quantity thought of as several separate things. "The number of vegetables served was unusual."

ample—should be used when referring to immaterial or abstract things. "Ample housing facilities."
plenty—should be used when referring to concrete things. "Plenty of houses."

and—redundant when used in a series ending with *etc*.
Should not be used for *or* in a series. "Bags of goodies, such as cookies, candies, and (not *or*) nuts."
See *try*.

and/or—should be avoided except in business or legal documents unless there are three alternatives (one, or the other, or both).

and which, and who, but which, but who—should be used only when a *which* or *who* clause precedes it in a sentence. "The dog which saved the child and which belongs to our neighbor . . ."

anecdote—a short account of an incident.
story—a well-organized account of several incidents that lead to a climax.
tale—a loosely organized account of a series of incidents.

anger—sudden, violent displeasure.
indignation—righteous anger.
resentment—sullen, brooding anger.

announce—to tell what is presumably not known. "They announced the baby's birth."
declare—to state a fact or opinion. "They declared that John had made the suggestion."

annoy—to disturb to the point of irritation. "The children's bickering annoyed me."
exasperate—to excite to hot anger. "His utter stubbornness exasperated me."
provoke—to arouse annoyance. "His repeated tardiness provoked the teacher."

another—redundant when used with *too* or *also*.
Should be followed by *than* (not *from*). "Another car than the one you saw."
In expressing alternatives, *one* should be used with *another*, and *some* should be used with *other*. "One (not *some*) way or another." "Some (not *one*) way or other."

ante—before. "ante bellum."
anti—against. "antitoxin."

anticipate—to look forward with emotion of some kind. "He anticipated with pleasure the visit from his grandchildren."
expect—to look forward to something uncertain. "I expect him to come."

anxious—is associated with worry or concern. "John was anxious to start home."
eager—is associated with desire or anticipation. "John was eager to go to college."

any, every—may be compounded in such words as *anyone, anyhow, anyway, everyone*, except that these words are written as two words when stress is on the individual element. "Anyone can spell simple words." "Any one of you can spell correctly if you try." "Everyone came on time." "Every one of them was there by eight o'clock."

any one, none—should be used to designate one of three or more persons or things.
either, neither—should be used to designate one of two persons or things, not each of the two.
See *any*.

anywhere, somewhere (not *any place, some place*).

apparent—what seems to be real. "There was an apparent error in the figures."
evident—what both seems and is real. "That they did not board the plane was evident."

appendix—see *-ex, -ix*.

appreciate—place a high value on (not *to understand*).
Should not be modified by *very much, greatly*, etc.
Should be followed by a noun, not by a *that* clause.

approximately—nearly equal to. *About* should be used instead of *approximately* when meaning merely *in the neighborhood of*.

apropos—with respect to. Should usually be used with *of*. "Apropos of his remarks."

apt—implies habitual tendency. "Apt to be late."

liable—implies the threat of unfavorable results. "Liable to get hurt."

likely—implies simply probability. "Likely to want to go."

area—should not be overused to mean *department, field, line*, etc.

around—near to, on every side (not *about* or *nearly*).

arrogant—objectionably overbearing.

haughty—showing evidence of having a higher opinion of oneself than of others.

as—should not be overworked as a substitute for *because, for, since, while*, etc., unless the meaning is instantly clear. "Since Christmas falls on Sunday, the meeting will be held on the following Monday." "As I passed the house, he came out."
Should not be used to mean *such as* or *for example*.

as (conj.)—in the same or similar manner. Should be used to introduce a clause. "He arrived on time as he said he would."

like (prep.)—in the same or similar manner. Should be used to introduce a phrase. "He carried an umbrella like mine."

as . . . as—should be used in affirmative statements; *so . . . as*, in negative statements. "As lovely as a flower." "Not so cold as yesterday."

as far as, so far as—should be written as three words. Should not ordinarily be introduced by *in*.

as follows—should always be used in the singular, even when several items are being introduced.

as if, as though—may be used interchangeably to express a supposition, and should almost always be followed by a past conditional verb (rather than by the present). "It looks as if (or *as though*) he were going to win."
Should not be used to introduce a direct object or predicate noun clause. *That* should be used. "He felt that (not *as if*) he should go."

as to—may be used at the beginning of a sentence when mentioning something specific. "As to his manner, it was very abrupt."
Should not be substituted for *for, about,* or *of*. "Plans for (not *as to*) his future. . . ."
Should not be used before *how, when, where,* or *whether* unless preceded by a verb. "The question concerning (not *as to*) whether he was a citizen did not come up." "The question of (not *as to*) his fitness for the position." When not preceded by a verb, *of* should be used instead of *as to*.

ascertain—to find out by investigation (not *to discover* or *understand*).

assent—see *agree*.

assert—see *allege*.

assume—take for granted but have some assurance. "I assume you will be there."

presume—take for granted and actually believe (stronger than *assume*). "I presume you will need more information on the case."

suppose—accept as a probability. "I suppose I will have to go alone."

assure—should not be used to mean *promise*.

at—implies a specific geographical location. "At Lake James."

in—usually means within the boundaries of a certain area. "In Chicago."

into—implies motion from one place or situation to another. "He turned into our lane."

on—implies geographical location on a wide or long area. "On Front Street." "On the Florida coast."

at all—redundant when used after *any*. "He could not see any."

attempt—exertion toward an end, while seeing the possibility of failure. "His attempt to follow a rigid diet."

effort—exertion toward an end, while looking forward to success. "His untiring effort to complete his degree by June."

attendance *at* (not *in*) school.

aught—anything, any part. "They could see aught of the campsite."

naught—the arithmetic cipher (zero), nothing. "A naught was placed in the units column."

authority *on* (not *in*) a subject. "He is an authority on birds."

averse—see *adverse*.

avocation—an activity carried on regularly for recreation rather than money. "Her avocation was gardening."

vocation—an occupation carried on regularly upon which one depends for a living. "Her vocation was teaching."

aware—conscious of things perceived outside oneself. "He was aware that they were watching him."

conscious—aware of one's own thoughts and actions. "He was conscious of his own shortcomings."

bad—of poor quality or unsatisfactory nature.

evil—morally bad.

wicked—bad both in practice and in principle.

balance—the remaining part when one amount of money is taken from another. "Balance of the account."

remainder—the remaining part of something, including mathematical material. "Remainder of the school fund."

rest—the remaining part of something other than mathematical material. "Rest of the day."

bank—the right-hand bank of a river is the one on the right when a person looks downstream.

barely, hardly, scarcely—imply negation and therefore should not be used with a negative.
A clause that follows one of these words should be introduced by *when* (not *than*). "I had hardly left the house when he called."

B.C.—see *A.D.*

bear—to hold up a burden that taxes the endurance. "He bore the burden bravely."

endure—to bear a burden grimly over a period of time. "He endured the pain for weeks."

because—redundant when used after *the reason is*. *That* should be used instead. "The reason he failed was that (not *because*) he could not read."
Should be used only to state a cause; *for* (conj.) should be used when merely offering evidence. "He failed because he could not read." "He failed, for we saw his grade."
See *as*.

begin—to do the first part of an action. "To begin to make a dress."

inaugurate—to initiate something under favorable circumstances. "To inaugurate a new plan."

start—to begin a course of action. "To start to the grocery."

behavior—one's actions in the presence of others. "The children were complimented on their behavior."

conduct—outward action, including the moral aspects of behavior. "His conduct under trying circumstances was admirable."

behind (not *in back of*).

believe—to accept as true.

below—less in amount. "The enrollment was below that of last year."

under—less in position. "The papers were under his briefcase."

besides (not *beside*)—when meaning *in additon to*.

biannual—twice a year.
biennial—once in two years.
semiannual—twice a year at six-month intervals.

big—large in size. "A big box."
great—large in degree or importance. "A great incentive."
large—large in size or quantity. "A large amount."

bloom—the flower itself. "Lilac blooms."
blossom—usually the flower that promises fruit. "Apple blossoms."

book—refers especially to the contents. "A book about the Civil War."
volume—refers especially to the physical make-up. "A history written in four volumes."

both—should be followed by *and*, not by *as well as*.

both—refers to two objects considered together.
each—refers to two or more objects considered separately.

brief—refers to time alone.
short—refers to time and space.

broad—refers to the expanse of space between limits.
wide—refers to the distance between those limits.

broad-leaved—is preferable to *broad-leafed*.

business—an interest pursued regularly for income.
commerce—business on a large scale.
employment—work done for pay in the service of another.
profession—business that requires professional training.
trade—business of buying and selling goods.

but—should not be used to mean *only*. "He saved only (not *but*) a few."
   See *cannot but* and *else*.

but that—should not be preceded or followed by *not* when it has a negative implication. "I do not doubt that (not *but that*) . . ." "How do you know that they will be (not *but that they will not be*) there?"

by means of— *means of* is usually superfluous.

calculate—to ascertain by using mathematical processes. "The scientist calculated the speed of the rocket."
compute—to make an accurate calculation on the basis of given numerical data. "The banker computed the interest."
estimate—to make a rough and approximate calculation. "The architect estimated the cost of the building."

can—denotes ability or power to act. "Surely you can make a call."
may—denotes permission or sanction to act. "You may make a call if you don't talk too much."

cannot but (not *cannot help but*)—can do nothing except. "I cannot but believe he is honest."
cannot help—cannot avoid. "I cannot help thinking he is honest." Do not use another negative in the sentence.
cannot seem to— *seem unable to* is preferable.

capacity—see *ability*

capital (noun)—city in which the seat of government is located.
capitol—the capitol building occupied by Congress or a state legislature.

careful—attempting to act wisely and responsibly. "A careful worker."
cautious—being careful but being timid or fearful. "A cautious driver."

case—specific instance, when used in the sense of illustration. "In the case of John Brown."
example—illustration, often in the moral and intellectual field. "An example of his honesty."
instance—an example which demonstrates or proves a point. "An instance of his stubbornness."
specimen—an example that is representative of a class or whole. "A specimen of quartz."

catalog—is preferable to *catalogue*.

cause—should not be used with *due to*. (Redundant) "The cause of his cold was (not *was not due to*) his having sat in a draft."

cause—that which produces an effect.
reason—the mind's argument for an act, conclusion, etc.

cause *for* an action. "The cause for rejoicing."
cause *of* a result. "The cause of her happiness."

cautious—see *careful*.

censure—to find fault with, to criticize as wrong. "Censure them for their ill manners."
criticize—to examine and judge as a critic, either favorably or unfavorably. "Criticize a work of art."

certainty—a fact or truth. "The certainty that day will follow night."
reality—state of being in existence. "His dream became a reality."

character—what a person is.
reputation—what a person is considered to be.

chief—highest in rank or title.
main—greatest in extent, quantity, or size.
principal—highest in importance.

choice—see *alternative*.

circa (or its abbreviations, *c.* or *cir.*)—about. May be used with dates but not with eras or centuries.

claim—see *allege*.

close—to bring to an end by not continuing. "That chapter of his life was closed."
complete—to bring to a state of entirety. "The work on the manuscript was completed."
conclude—to bring to a suitable or desired point. "They concluded the program with a song."
end—to come to a final issue. "The search was ended."
finish—to arrive at the end of. "He finished reading the book."

coefficient, cooperate, coordinate, etc.—such words are preferably written without the hyphen.

colleague—see *ally*.

commerce—see *business*.

common—belonging to or shared by more than one person. "Common effort."
mutual—reciprocal action or property. "Mutual benefit."

compare *to*—should be used when showing similarities of things in the same class. "Compare one book cover to another."
compare *with*—should be used when showing differences as well as similarities of dissimilar things. "Compare a fenced yard with a prison."

contrast—show striking differences. "The black contrasted with the pink in the decorations."
compatible *with* (not *to*).
complement (verb)—to make complete.
compliment (verb)—to praise.
complete—see *close*.
complex—having many related and connected parts.
complicated—so complex as to be hard to understand.
comply—see *agree*.
compose—to form by putting together two or more elements. "This alloy is composed of nickel and copper."
comprise—to be made up of a number of parts of a whole. "Those three sections comprise Chapter II."
compute—see *calculate*.
conceited—having a superior opinion of one's own ability and qualities.
egotistical—being more interested in oneself than in others.
conclude—see *close*.
concur—see *agree*.
confess—see *admit*.
confirm—to establish something which was doubtful. "To confirm a rumor."
establish—to prove the truth and have it accepted as true. "The exact date was established from the record in the family Bible."
substantiate—to prove on the basis of evidence. "The report was substantiated."
connect *by*—should be used when means are emphasized. "The towns are connected by a state highway."
connect *with*—should be used when relationship is emphasized. "The outbreak of typhoid fever is connected with the lack of a pure water supply."
conscious—see *aware*.
consensus—should not be used with *of opinion*. (Redundant) "The consensus of the committee was that . . ."
consent—see *agree*.
consider—should not be followed by *as* or *to be* when used in the sense of judge or regard. "They considered the plan successful (not *to be successful*)."
considerable—rather large in extent or worth (not in amount). "They needed considerable patience (not *considerable money*) in carrying out the project."
consume—should not be used with *completely* or *totally*. (Redundant)
contact—should be used as a verb only in technical language or to mean *touch* or *come together*. "I telephoned (not *contacted*) the president."
contain—to hold within fixed limits. "The jar contains one gallon."
include—to contain as a part of the whole. "The book includes a chapter on poetry."
content (noun)—should be used as an abstract noun in amounts. "Content of a speech." "Vitamin content of a meal."
contents (noun)—should be used as a more concrete noun, meaning that which is contained. "The contents of a bottle."
continual—occurring with interruption, but always going on. "Continual demands for money."
continuous—occurring without interruption while it continues. "Continuous noise."
continue—should not be followed by *on*. (Redundant)

contrast—see *compare*.
control—govern, direct, regulate. "He controlled the price of the book."
manage—administer, handle. "He managed the business."
correct—see *accurate*.
correct (verb)—to make a thing right according to a standard. "He corrected his answers."
rectify—to make a wrong thing right. "He rectified the error."
correspond *to*—match, be analogous to.
correspond *with*—agree with, be in harmony with (not as closely corresponding as *correspond to*).
could—see *would*.
council—an assembly summoned or convened for consultation, advice, etc. "The council passed Henry's motion."
counsel—advice, opinion, exchange of opinion, consultation. "They needed counsel before making a decision."
criticize—see *censure*.
damage—applies to property only.
injury—applies generally to persons, feelings, reputation, etc.
data—is plural except when used to apply to a body of information as a unit.
date—prepositions used with dates should show the meaning clearly. "In 1961-1962." "In 1961 and 1962." "Between 1961 and 1963." "From 1961 to 1963 (not *from 1961-1963*)." "The year 1962 (not *of 1962*)."
dates (verb) *from* (not *back to*).
deal—should not be used to mean business arrangement.
a great deal—should be used sparingly.
deceitful—full of deceit or trickery. "He was so deceitful he could not be trusted with anything."
deceptive—tending to deceive or mislead. "His explanation of the error was deceptive."
declare—see *announce*
delimit—to fix or mark the limits of, to bound.
limit—to confine within bounds, to apply limits.
delusion—see *allusion*.
depreciate—should not be followed by the words *in value*. (Redundant)
design—an idea of something to be done and the means of doing it. "Design for the poster."
plan—detailed method of working out the design. "Plan for the new house."
purpose—a definite idea to be carried out. "The purpose in holding the meeting."
die *of* or *from* (not *with*).
differ *from*—be different.
differ *with*—disagree with.
difference—unlikeness.
distinction—mental recognition of unlikeness.
different *from* (not *than*), except when it introduces an understood clause. "He reacted in a different way than ever before."
dimensions—expresses size.
proportions—expresses a relationship.
discover—to bring to light something new but already in existence. "To discover another chemical element."
invent—to devise something new. "To invent a knitting machine."
discreet—having discretion.
discrete—divided into distinct and separate parts.
dispense *with*—to do away with. "He dispensed with the red tape."

dispose *of*—to get rid of. "He disposed of his collection of antiques."

distinction—see *difference*.

do, did—should seldom be used as an auxiliary for emphasis.

dogmatic—thinking one's own way of doing something is the only right way.

opinionated—thinking one's own judgment is right, and making it known.

doubt *that*—should be used with questions and negative statements when there is no real doubt. "I do not doubt that he will go."

doubt *whether* (or *that*)—should be used with affirmative statements when doubt exists. "I doubt whether he will go."

due (adj.) to—caused by. Should modify a noun or pronoun. "His success was due to his outgoing personality." "They were not able to go because of (not *due to*) the rain."

owing to (compound prep.)—because of, on account of. Should be used to introduce adverbial phrases modifying verbs. "He lost money owing to the rerouting of the highway."
See *cause*.

duplicate—an exact copy. Redundant when used with *copy*. "He has a duplicate (not *duplicate copy*) of the contract."

each—should be considered singular except when it immediately follows a plural noun or pronoun. "Each of them has a bicycle." "They each have a bicycle."
See *among*.

each other—should be used when only two things are referred to

one another—should be used when more than two things are referred to.

eager—see *anxious*.

earliest—first in time. "The earliest edition."
first—ahead of the others. "The first to leave."
latest—most recent. "The latest issue of a magazine."
last—final. "The last person in line."

effect—see *affect*.

effective—producing actual desired results. "Effective laws."

effectual—producing desired results but with the idea of finality. Used with things, not persons. "Effectual means of killing the weeds."

efficient—producing desired results through the exercise of energy. Used usually with persons. "An efficient secretary."

effort—see *attempt*.

e.g.—should not usually be italicized.

egoist—one who thinks always of himself.

egotist—one who is self-important and talks much of himself.

either—see *any one*.

element—a part which goes into the making of the whole.
factor—an element that produces a result.
phase—a stage in the development of something, an aspect of something that varies.

else—should not be used with *but*. "No one but (not *no one else but*) John went to the show."
Should not be used with *or*. "He has to be there or (not *or else*) be marked absent."

emigrate—to leave a country to settle elsewhere.
immigrate—to come into a country to settle there.

employment—see *business*.

enclose—preferable to inclose.

end—see *aim*.

ended—used in phrases that express past time. "It was common during the period ended in 1918."

ending—used in present or future phrases. "It will be completed in the decade ending in 1990."

endure—see *bear*.

enough (noun)—should be followed by an infinitive rather than by *that* or *so that*. "He had enough to be able to give some away."

enough—is preferable when only amount is considered. "Enough money."

sufficient—is preferable when quality or kind is considered. "Sufficient light."

enter *into* an agreement.

enter *on* or *upon* an undertaking or career.

entire—should not be used with *throughout*. (Redundant) "The noise continued throughout the performance."

equally—should not be follwed by *as*. (Redundant)

-er, -re—words like *caliber, center,* and *theater* should end with *-er* rather than *-re*.

especially—particularly, "He was especially fitted for the job."

specially—in a special manner, "He was specially trained for the job."

essential—urgently necessary. "Medication is essential if he is to survive."

necessary—needed as a requirement. "Winter clothes are necessary in that climate."

requisite—required for a certain purpose. "Extensive travel in a country is requisite to an understanding of its problems."

establish—see *confirm*.

estimate—see *calculate*.

etc.—should be avoided in formal writing. Should be followed by a comma only when it would be if written out as *and so forth*.

evaluation—action of placing a value on something, or estimating its worth. "The committee's evaluation of the property."

valuation—a statement of the calculated value of something, an appraisal. "The valuation placed on the property for tax purposes."

event—happening of significance.

incident—one of the minor happenings in something of which it is a part.

ever—compounds of *ever* (such as *however, whatever, whichever,* etc.) should not be used as interrogatives for emphasis. "Who (not *whoever*) said that?" "What (not *whatever*) made you do that?"

every—see *among*.

everyone—see *any*.

evident—see *apparent*.

evil—see *bad*.

ex- —should ordinarily be used, as a prefix meaning formerly, only with single words and should be attached by a hyphen. With compound terms, like *attorney general*, the word *formerly* should be used instead of *ex-*.

-ex, -ix—the plural of words ending in these letters should be formed with *-ices* if they are used purely scientifically or technically. If they are trade names or are used in a popular sense, the English endings, *-exes* or *-ixes*, should be used.

example—see *case*.

exasperate—see *annoy*.

exceedingly—very greatly.
excessively—too greatly.
excepting—should be used only to mean *not including*. When an exception is not to be made, *not excepting* or *not excepted* should be used. "All excepting children are invited." "Children not excepted."
expect—see *anticipate*.
explain—to clear up something not understood. "Explain a theorem in geometry."
interpret—to bring out the meaning. "To interpret a technical report on radar."
extent to which—see *to the extent that*.
fact—something actually true, not merely something thought to be true. Should not be used with *true*. (Redundant)
the fact that—*that* can usually be used alone. "He was conscious (of the fact) that . . ."
factor—should not be overused in the sense of *circumstance, element, influence,* etc.
See *element*.
fail a test.
fame—public estimation, reputation.
renown—exalted fame, illustrious reputation.
far—see *as far as* and *in so far as*.
farther—at a greater distance. "He had to drive farther than the others."
further—to a greater degree. "He mentioned nothing further."
feature—should not be used as a verb to mean *give special prominence to*.
feel—see *believe*.
few—a negative term meaning *not many*. "Few people attended the meeting."
a few—a positive term meaning *several*. "A few men attended the PTA meeting."
the few—a specific term. "The few who attended the meeting."
fewer, fewest—should be used with things measured by number. "Fewer dollars." "Fewer acres."
less, least—should be used with things measured by degree, amount, or value. "Less money." "'less acreage."
field—should seldom be used to mean *area, class,* or *department*.
figuratively—expressing one thing in terms ordinarily used for another.
literally—expressing something in words used primarily for that purpose.
find—to discover by effort. "John found the billfold he had lost."
locate—to discover the location. "We located the home of our friend."
finish—see *close*.
first—is preferable to *firstly,* even when *secondly* is used. See *earliest*.
first two—is usually more accurate than *two first,* as there are not ordinarily two or more first things or people.
following—should not be used as a preposition when referring to time. "The monument was built five years after (not *following*) the erection of the courthouse."
follows—the term *as follows* should always be used in the singular, even when several items are being introduced.
for (conj.)—see *as, as to,* and *because*.
for example—should be used when referring to typical or representative cases or facts. "For example, the requirements for certification."

for instance—should be used only when referring to illustrative cases or facts. "For instance, the dress worn by the hostess."
foreword—preface, introductory remark.
forward—advanced toward what is in front.
former—the first of only two persons or things previously mentioned.
latter—the second of only two persons or things previously mentioned.
Neither word should be used to refer to a pronoun. When referring to more than two persons or things, *first* and *last* should be used.
forward—toward what is before or in front. "From this year forward."
Is preferable to *forwards* except when referring to a definite direction in contrast with others. "The toy moves only forwards."
fourth—one of four equal parts considered as a part of the whole. "A fourth of the apples."
quarter—one of four equal parts considered as a measured section or division. "A quarter of an hour."
fraction—should not be used to mean a *portion* or *a little*.
free *of* responsibility.
freed *from* responsibility.
freshman (adj.)—should be used to modify either singular or plural terms. "Freshman students."
further—see *farther*.
genius—exceptional creative intellectual capacity.
talent—exceptional mental ability in a certain field, usually ability that has been developed through training.
goods—always considered to be plural.
got—*have got* should not be used to mean *possess* or *have*.
graduate *from*.
graduated *by* (not *at*).
half—when written in words, *a foot and a half* is preferable to *one and a half feet*.
a half a day—omit one *a*. "Half a day," or "A half day."
half as large—is preferable to *twice as small*.
hanged—put to death.
hung—suspended from above.
happen—take place, occur. "The accident happened."
take place—take place by design. "The wedding took place."
hardly—see *barely*.
hardly ever—is preferable to *almost never*.
haughty—see *arrogant*.
healthful—conducive to good health. "The climate is healthful."
healthy—enjoying good health. "A healthy person."
wholesome—good for a person. "Wholesome surroundings."
help—see *but*.
hereto, herewith—redundant when used with such terms as *attached* or *enclosed*.
his—the possessive form of *one* when *one* refers to a person. "One would not want his family harmed."
Is used in place of *his or her*.
home—dwelling place of a family.
house—a building for residence.
Honorable, Reverend—should be preceded by *the* if only the last name of the person follows. "The Reverend Smith." "Honorable Jon Q. Smith."
hope—should be used in the singular if one thing is being hoped for. "I have hope of being able to attend."

In the passive, *it* should be used, "The trip is what, it is hoped, will . . ." not "The trip is what is hoped will . . ."

however—should be placed in the sentence where it shows the contrasting emphasis desired.
Redundant when used with *but*.

humble—poor, applied to persons.
lowly—poor, usually applied to conditions.

identical—see *alike*.

identified *with*—should not be used for *associated with* or *employed by*.

if—should be used to introduce conditions or conditional ideas. "They can go if the weather clears."
Should not be used to mean *when* or *where*. "Where (not *if*) differences were found, an attempt was made to investigate further."
See *as if* and *whether*.

if and when—one or the other of these two words should usually be omitted.

if any—ordinarily *if any* in sentences like the following is unnecessary. "Mark the errors on the test," not "Mark the errors, if any, on the test."

ignorant *in*—uninformed. "She is ignorant in the subject."
ignorant *of*—unaware. "She is ignorant of his interest in her work."

ill *with* a disease.

illusion—see *allusion*.

imbue *with*.

impatient *at* actions or characteristics.
impatient *with* persons.

imply—to suggest. A noun clause following imply should be introduced by *that*. "The president implied that he had to leave on Tuesday."

infer—to draw a certain meaning from a remark or action. "The president inferred from what I said that he had to leave on Tuesday."

impressed *by* or *with*.

in—*within* is preferable in expressions of time like the following. "I can get to Chicago within (not *in*) five hours."

inasmuch as—is preferably written as two words.

inaugurate—see *begin*.

incident—see *event*.

include—see *contain*.

incompatible *with*—incapable of existing together. "Serenity is incompatible with turmoil."

inconsistent *with*—unsuitable to be considered together. "His conduct is inconsistent with his teachings."

increase *in*.

index—see *-ex, -ix*.

indignation—see *anger*.

individual—a single human being.
party—a body of persons. Only in legal actions or affairs may *party* be used to mean one of those who make up one side of the action.
Neither of these words should be used casually to mean *person*.

infer—see *imply*.

inform—see *acquaint*.

information—knowledge of certain facts.
knowledge—the whole body of facts that one knows.
news—knowledge of recent and timely facts.

in order to—the words *in order* should be omitted unless necessary to the meaning. "A child must be born before December 1 to (not *in order to*) be eligible."

in order that—should be followed by *may* or *might* (not by *can* or *could*).

in regard to, with regard to, as regards (not *in regards to* or *with regards to*).
Avoid using when *in*, *about*, etc. can be used. "That is a good story about (not *in regard to*) pets."

in search *of* (not *for*).

inside—should not be followed by *of* when it means *within*. "The gift was placed inside the box."

in so far as—*in* is usually superfluous.

instance—see *case* and *for instance*.

instinct—the characteristic that animals have which serves them in place of the ability to reason.

intuition—the immediate mental recognition of a fact or situation without the use of any reasoning process.

intention *of doing* or *to do*.

interfere *in* something.
interfere *with* a person.

interpret—see *explain*.

interstate—between states.
intrastate—within a state.

into—see *at*.

in the light of—the word *the* should always be included. "He looked at the problem in the light of its possibilities."

intuition—see *instinct*.

invent—see *discover*.

irregardless—omit the *ir*.

irritate—see *annoy*.

issue—a point in debate or controversy (not *discussion* or *matter*).

its—possessive form of *it*.
it's—means *it is*.

joined—should not be used with *together*. (Redundant)

just—precisely, barely, exactly (not *completely, perfectly,* or *very*). "It was very (not *just*) lovely."

kind of, type of—should not be followed by *a* or *an*.
Should be followed by a singular noun unless the plural idea is especially strong. "This type of machine is new." "That kind of data are needed."

knowledge—see *information*.

last—see *earliest*.
latest—see *earliest*.
latter—should not be used in general expressions. "The last (not *the latter*) part of the book."
See *former*.

least—see *fewer*.

lent—past tense of *lend*, except that in business transactions, when referring to money, *loaned* is correct.

less—see *fewer*.

liable—see *apt*.

light—see *in the light of*.

like—see *as*.

likely—see *apt*.

limit—see *delimit*.

literature—should be used to refer to recognized literary writing, not to printed materials in general. "The advertising material (not *literature*) was received in May."
little—should be used in referring to quantity or amount.
small—should be used in referring to extent, importance, quality, or size.
loaned—see *lent*.
locate—see *find*.
lowly—see *humble*.
main—see *chief*.
majority—the greater of two parts making up a whole.
minority—the smaller of two parts making up a whole.
plurality—the largest portion, but not more than half of the whole.
manage—see *control*.
manikin—an anatomical model.
mannequin—a person who models costumes.
many—refers to number. "How many doughnuts should I buy?"
much—refers to quantity. "How much applesauce should I buy?"
materialize—should not be used to mean *fulfill, happen,* or *develop*.
may—expresses a strong possibility. See *can*.
might—expresses a remote possibility.
menace—only persons or large things may menace. "The tidal wave menaced the homes on the coast."
threaten—persons, or things of any size, may threaten. "The teacher threatened to punish the children."
miner—one who mines.
minor—one who is under legal age.
minority—see *majority*.
mm.—in referring to films or slides, this abbreviation for millimeter is acceptable. It should be written with a space after the figure, as in "16 mm."
more than—is preferable to *over* when expressing excess in amount or quantity. "More than five dollars."
most—see *almost*.
much—see *many*.
must—past tense of *had to*.
mutual—see *common*.
natural—existing in or by nature of. "Natural dye."
normal—conforming to a standard of nature. "Normal rainfall."
naught—see *aught*.
necessary—see *essential*.
neither—see *anyone*.
never—should not be used to mean *not*. "He was supposed to go to market that day, but he did not go (not *he never went*)."
news—see *information*.
nice—delicately made, precise (not *agreeable* or *pleasant*).
no . . . or— when a negative precedes a series of alternatives and applies to each, *or* (not *nor*) should precede the last item in the series. "No man, woman, or child can live through it."
none—see *any one*.
normal—see *natural*.

no sooner *than* (not *before, until,* or *when*). "No sooner had he left than the phone rang."
no such—should not be followed by *a* or *an*. "No such animal."
notify—see *acquaint*.
number—see *amount* and *quantity*.
object—see *aim*.
obsolescent—going out of use.
obsolete—no longer in use.
obtain—see *acquire*.
off—Should not be followed by *of*. (Redundant)
on the contrary—usually introduces something contrary to what has preceded.
on the other hand—never introduces something conflicting with what has preceded.
one—see *another* and *his*.
one another—see *each other*.
only—see *alone*.
opinionated—see *dogmatic*.
or—see *else* and *no . . . or*.
oral—expressed in spoken words.
verbal—expressed in words, either written or spoken.
order—see *in order that*.
originate *in* a place or thing.
originate *with* a person.
otherwise *than* (not *but*). "He could not do otherwise than go."
ought—expresses a stronger obligation than *should*. "You ought to call him at once." "You should plan to see him while you are in town."
outside—should not be followed by *of* when it means *besides* or *except*.
overcome *by* smoke.
overcome *with* remorse.
owing to—see *due to*.
pair—the plural should be used when speaking of more than one. "Five pairs of stockings."
palate—roof of the mouth.
palette—a painter's color board.
pallet—a small humble bed.
par—should be avoided in literary writing, but may be used in business.
parcel (verb)—distribute. "Supplies were parcelled (not *partialed*) out to the flood victims."
part—less than all of a thing. "He spent part of the afternoon at the library."
portion—an allotted part. "His portion of the estate."
partial—see *parcel*.
partially—to a limited degree.
partly—as a part of a whole.
partner—see *ally*.
party—see *individual*.
past—should not be used to mean *just gone by* in expressions involving more than one unit of time. "The past week." "The last (not *past*) three days."
people—persons considered as a group. "The American people."
persons—persons considered as individuals. "Six persons were injured."

per—should not be used with English words except in business and economics. "He made at least one trip a (not *per*) year."
Should not be used to mean *concerning* or *according to*. "Concerning (not *per*) the matter." "According to (not *per*) your instructions."
May be used in Latin terms like *per diem* and *percent*, that are now accepted as English.

per capita—should be used only in reference to a certain method of sharing property.
Should not be used to mean *for each person*. "The cost for each (not *per capita*) was $5.25."

percent—should be written as one word and should not be followed by a period.

percentage—proportion on the basis of 100 parts. Is often used instead of *percent* when no definite number is referred to.

pertinent—fitted and adapted to a proposed purpose. "His remarks were pertinent to the purposes of the meeting."

relevant—logically related to a subject. "Only relevant data should be included in the study."

phase—see *element*.

plan—see *design*.

plenty—see *ample*.

plurality—see *majority*.

portion—see *part*.

postal card—official mailing card with postage stamp printed on it.

postcard—unofficial mailing card without postage stamp printed on it.

posted—should be used to mean *informed* only when referring to business or commercial matters.

postpone—see *defer*.

practicable—capable of being put into practice.

practical—useful in actual practice.

preference—see *alternative*.

presently—before long, soon (not *at present*). "I expect to complete the book presently." "I am working on something else at present."

presume—see *assume*.

principal—see *chief*.

principal—one who is highest in authority, importance, or rank.

principle—fundamental truth or rule of action.

profession—see *business*.

proposal—a suggestion offered for acceptance.

proposition—a suggestion offered for consideration. May be used as a business and commercial term for *proposal*.

proved—is preferable to *proven* except when used as an adjective. "He has proved his worth." "Proven worth."

provoke—see *annoy*.

purpose—see *design*.

quantity—an amount which can be measured by a standard. Should not be used to mean *number*.

quarter—in referrring to time of day, *a quarter to* (not *of*) should be used.
See *fourth*.

question *concerning* (not *asking*).

quite—means *entirely* or *positively* (not *rather* or *very*). "The attempt was quite successful."

range from . . . to (not *up to*)—would not be used unless figures are given for both extremes. "The scores range from 42 to 98."

rare—uncommon.

scarce—hard to obtain.

unique—only one of its kind.

rarely if ever (not *rarely ever*).

reaction—a counter tendency. "A chemical reaction." Should seldom be used to mean *response, impression,* or *opinion*. "What was her response (not *reaction*) to the comment?"

real—actual, genuine (not *very*, or *extremely*).

reason—see *because*.

rectify—see *correct*.

re-enforce—enforce again.

reinforce—strengthen.

refer to—see *allude to*.

regard—see *in regard to*.

relevant—see *pertinent*.

remainder—see *balance*.

reputation—see *character*.

requisite—see *essential*.

resentment—see *anger*.

respectfully—worth respect.

respectively—in the order designated.

revenge—see *avenge*.

said, same, such—should not be substituted for a noun or pronoun except in legal documents. "They will pack the dishes and ship them (not *ship same*)."

sanitarium—institution giving medical treatment.

sanitorium—health resort.

search—see *in search of*.

seem—should not be used unnecessarily. "Appears (not *seems to appear*) incidental."

seldom or never, seldom if ever (not *seldom or ever*, or *seldom ever*).

semi—a word which has *semi* as a prefix usually written without the hyphen.

semiannual—see *biannual*.

settle—should not be used to mean *pay* unless there has been a controversy concerning the matter.

shall, will—to denote simple futurity or condition, *shall* or *should* should be used in the first person, *will* or *would* in the second and third persons; to denote determination or command, willingness, or promise, the opposite should be used.
In *that* clauses expressing desire or inclination, *shall* or *should* should be used in all persons. "I intend that he shall . . ." "I intended that he should . . ."

short—see *brief*.

should—is used to express condition or obligation. "If it should snow, we will not make the trip." "I should go and care for him."
See *ought* and *shall*.

similar—see *alike*.

since—should not be used to express cause or time unless the meaning is instantly obvious. "Because (not *since*) he was ill, he did not attend many meetings."
See *ago* and *as*.

size (noun)—should be followed by *of* in expressions like "that size of cake."

Either *size* or *sized* may be combined with another word to form a hyphenated compound adjective, depending upon the meaning intended. *Sized* is the more commonly used and usually conveys the idea that some action has been involved. "Medium-sized eggs" suggests the eggs have been sorted; "medium-size eggs" suggests eggs of a medium size.

small—see *little*.

so—to such a degree, in such manner (not *in order that*). Is usually followed by *that*. "He studied so late that he overslept next morning."
In connecting independent clauses, *and so* (not *so*) should be used. "She brought some eggs, and so (not *so only*) we baked a cake."

so-called—should not be used unnecessarily.

so far as—see *as far as*.

some—see *another*.

someone—see *anyone*.

some place—see *anywhere*.

specially—see *especially*.

specimen—see *case*.

splendid—shining, brilliant (not *fine*, not a term of praise).

start—see *begin*.

stationary (adj.)—fixed in position.

stationery (noun)—writing paper.

story—see *anecdote*.

subject to—see *addicted to*.

subscribe *for* a magazine.
subscribe *to* a fund.

substantiate—see *confirm*.

such—should be used with *as*, when followed by a relative clause. "He demanded such service as might be fitting for a king."
Should be used with *that* when followed by a result clause. "It was such a foggy day that we could not fly."
Should not be overworked as an expletive. "A very (not *such a*) good story."

such as—see *as* and *etc*.

suffer—see *bear*.

sufficient—see *enough*.

suppose—see *assume*.

surround *by* (not *with*).

synonymous *with*.

take place—see *happen*.

tale—see *anecdote*.

talent—see *genius*.

than—should not be used for *until* or *when* after *hardly* or *scarcely*. "He had hardly begun his talk when (not *than*) they left."

that—refers to things, animals, and people.

which—refers only to animals and things, or to a collective noun designating persons.

who—refers to people and, rarely, to animals.

that—should not be used to mean *in which, for which,* or *to which*. "They do it in the same way in which (not *that*) their parents did." "To the extent to which (not *that*) . . ."

that, which—when *that* is used with a preposition, the preposition should be placed at the end of the clause; when *which* is used, the preposition should precede it. "The conversation that they carried on." "The situation in which he found himself."
Either *that* or *which* may be used to introduce a restrictive clause, but *which* is usually used to introduce a non-restrictive clause. "The requirements that make it necessary." "The requirements which are listed below make it necessary."
See *but*.

that is—should be used only when what follows is an explanation of or the equivalent of what precedes. "They requested no gifts, that is, no gifts from that group of people."

the—should be repeated after *and* joining two titles when necessary to make clear whether one or two persons are being referred to. "The secretary and treasurer." "The secretary and the treasurer."
Should not be omitted where needed for clarity and easy reading. Telegraphic English is not acceptable in research.

therefor—for this, for that.

therefore—consequently.

though—see *although* and *as if*.

threaten—see *menace*.

through—should not be used to mean *finished*.

throughout—see *entire*.

thus—should be used with the present participle only when the participle modifies the subject of the preceding verb. "He remained calm, thus quieting the others."

to the extent that—should be used only with ideas of quantity.

too—see *another*.

too, very—should not be overworked.
May be used alone with adjectives, but with participles these words must be followed by *much, greatly, well,* or some similar word. "He was very well pleased."

toward (not *towards*).

trade—see *business*.

try—when a verb follows such words as *try*, it should ordinarily be in the form of an infinitive. "Try to (not *and*) help them." "If no purpose or effort is meant, *and* may be used.

type of—see *kind of*.

under—see *below*.

unique—see *rare*.

United States—the word *the* should be used before *United States*.

until—is more formal than *till*.
Should not be used for *where* or *before* after the words *hardly* and *scarcely*. "He had hardly arrived before (not *until*) the train started."
See *than*.

utilize—overworked for *use*.

valuable—of much value. "A valuable piece of property."

valued—of recognized or sentimental value. "A valued family heirloom."

valuation—see *evaluation*.

vary—see *range*.

verbal—see *oral*.

very—see *too*.

via—should be used to mean *by* or *by way of* only in connection with routes of travel.

vocation—see *avocation*.

volume—see *book*.

waiver—to relinquish a right.

waver—to hesitate, flicker.

what is . . . is, what are . . . are—the number of *what* should be kept consistent in a sentence. "What is needed is . . ." "What were good points were . . ."

when—should not be used to define a word. "Evaporation is (not *is when*) . . ."
See *than* and *where*.

whence—from what place. Redundant when preceded by *from*.

where—should not be used for *that* in an object clause. "I heard that (not *where*) Jones was appointed."
Should not be used to mean *when*. "A problem arises when (not *where*) members are absent."

whether—may be used either with or without *or not* or *or no*. *Or not* should be used when an alternative is stressed. "He couldn't decide whether to go." "They decided to go whether or not we joined the party."
Whether (not *if*) should be used when introducing a dependent clause following a verb like *see*, *know*, or *doubt*. "I doubt whether (not *if*) he can come." "Jackson attempted to find out whether (not *if*) there was a difference."
See *as to* and *if*.

which—should not be used when the antecedent includes an ordinal numeral or a superlative. "This is the third honor that (not *which*) he has received." "This is the coldest winter that (not *which*) we have had."
Should not be used instead of *that* after expletives. "It is the house that (not *which*) . . ."
See *and which*, *ever*, and *that*.

which, who—all references to a collective noun in a sentence should be introduced by the same relative pronoun. "The people who came early and about whom (not *which*) I told you."
See *and which*.

while—at the same time that, during, as long as (not *and*, *but*, *though*, *when*, etc.). "While they were in class, we prepared for the party." "Though (not *while*) they said they were ready, they kept us waiting."
Should not be used as a conjunction to express contrast or concession. "The house is on the left, and (not *while*) the barn is across the road."
See *as*.

whoever—see *ever*.

wholesome—see *healthful*.

whose—possessive form of *that*, *which*, and *who*.

wicked—see *bad*.

would—should be used to express habitual action. "He would take the same train every day."
Should be avoided as a conditional auxiliary. "The sample seems (not *would seem*) to be representative.
When *would* is used in the main clause, *could* (not *can*) should be used in the subordinate clause. "He would stop on the way if you could (not *can*) arrange to meet him."

yet—see *although*.

youth—young people in general. "The youth of the nation."

youths—specific young men. "The three well-behaved youths."

BIBLIOGRAPHY

Alexander, Carter, and Burke, Arvid J., *How to Locate Educational Information and Data*, Bureau of Publications Teachers College, Columbia University, New York, 1958, 419 pp.

Barzun, Jacques Martin, and Graff, Henry F., *The Modern Researcher*, Harcourt, Brace and World, Inc., New York, 1963, 386 pp.

Bernstein, Theodore M., *Watch Your Language*, Pocket Books, Inc., New York, 1965, 213 pp.

Best, John W., *Research in Education*, Prentice-Hall, Inc., Englewood Cliffs, N. J., 1959, 320 pp.

Cohen, Morris R., and Nagel, Ernest, *An Introduction to Logic*, Harcourt, Brace and World, New York, 1962, 225 pp.

Conant, James Bryant, *Science and Common Sense*, Yale University Press, New Haven, Conn., 1961, 344 pp.

Dugdale, Kathleen, *A Manual of Form for Theses and Term Reports*, The author, Bloomington, Ind., 1967, 59 pp. (Available at the Indiana University Bookstore, Bloomington.)

Follett, Wilson, *Modern American Usage*, Hill and Wang, New York, 1966, 436 pp.

Garrett, Henry Edward, *Statistics in Psychology and Education*, David McKay, New York, 1966, 491 pp.

Good, Carter V., *Essentials of Educational Research: Methodology and Design*, Appleton-Century-Crofts, New York, 1966, 429 pp.

Hockett, Homer Carey, *Critical Method in Historical Research and Writing*, The Macmillan Co., New York, 1955, 330 pp.

Kerlinger, Fred N., *Foundations of Behavioral Research*, Holt, Rinehart, and Winston, Inc., New York, 1964, 739 pp.

Krathwohl, David R., *How to Prepare a Research Proposal*, Syracuse University Bookstore, Syracuse, New York, 1966, 50 pp.

Nicholson, Margaret, *A Dictionary of American English Usage, Based on Fowler's Modern English Usage*, The New American Library of World Literature, Inc., New York, 1958, 671 pp.

Northrup, Filmer Stuart Cuckow, *The Logic of the Sciences and the Humanities*, Meridian Books, Inc., New York, 1959, 402 pp.

Perrin, Porter Gale, *Writer's Guide and Index to English*, Scott, Foresman and Co., Galena, Ill., 1965, 907 pp.

Roget, Peter Mark, *The New Roget's Thesaurus of the English Language*, G. P. Putnam Sons, New York, 1965, 552 pp.

Travers, Robert Morris William, *An Introduction to Educational Research*, The Macmillan Co., New York, 1964, 581 pp.

Van Dalen, Deobold B., and Meyer, William J., *Understanding Educational Research*, McGraw-Hill Book Co., New York, 1966, 525 pp.

Whitney, Frederick Lamson, *Elements of Research*, Prentice-Hall, Inc., New York, 1950, 539 pp.

Wilson, Edgar Bright, *An Introduction to Scientific Research*, McGraw-Hill Book Co., New York, 1960, 375 pp.

INDEX

Abbreviating, 472-474
Administrator, 98-99, 167
Adverbs, 389
Alphabetizing
    In series, 395
    Of bibliography, 326
Appendix, 327

Bibliography
    Alphabetizing, 326
    Bibliography cards, 62-66
    Filing notes, 78-80
    In final study, 324-326
    In proposal, 50
    Note-taking cards, 67-77
    Numbered bibliography, 289
    Temporary bibliography, 7
Body of the report, 291-304
Brackets, 484-486
Budget time, 254

Capitalization, 478-481
Carbon copies, 255, 351
Case studies, 125-128
Chapter numbers and titles, 240
Clarity, 356
"Closed" questions, 146
Coherence, 356
Comparison of data, 205, 397-405
Concluding chapter
    Conclusions, 319-321
    Recommendations, 322-323
    Summary, 317-318
Conclusions
    In proposal, 49
    In study, 319-321
Confidential material, 136, 183
Correcting, 344-349
Criticism, 346-347
Cross references, 290

Dash, 493-494
Data-gathering instruments, 97, 134-189
Data-processing, 107-108, 156-157
Dependent variable, 131
Descriptive research, 114-128, 215-220
Dictionary, 252
Directions
    On questionnaire, 150
    On tests, 163, 166
Division headings,
    In proposal, 48
    In study, 23, 238-241, 342-343

Effective writing, 353-526
Ellipses, 70, 277
Emphasis, 356
Experimental research, 129-133, 221-235
External validity, 20, 90, 208

Field of study, 7
Figures, 234, 305-313
    Form, 307
    In appendix, 308
    In first draft, 305
    Numbering, 308
    Titles, 310
Figures of speech, 441
Filing notes, 78-80
First draft, 249-328
    Body of the report, 291-314
    Concluding chapter, 315-318
    Finish and set aside before revising 330-331
    Footnotes, 283-290
    Good working conditions, 249-255
    Illustrative material, 305-314
    Introduction, 266-276
    Quoting, 277-282
    Review of related literature, 275-276
    Supplementary pages, 324-328
Follow-ups, 144
Footnotes, 283-290
    Form, 284-285
    In numbered bibliography, 289
    Numbering, 286
    To tables and figures, 287
Foreign words, 435, 448, 450-451
Formulas, 297

The gathering and handling of the data, 52-235
    Data obtained from others, 81-189
    Handling the data, 190-235
Grammar, 372-434
Guides to references, 52-54

Handling the data, 190-235
    Descriptive research, 215-220
    Experimental research, 221-235
    Historical research, 211-214
    Research in general, 190-210
Headings, 23, 48, 238-241, 342-343
Historical background, 268-269
Historical research, 109-113, 211-214

Home-made instruments, 164-166
Hyphenating, 462-471
Hypotheses
    First draft, 270-272, 321
    In proposal, 38-44
    Temporary hypotheses, 85-86
    Testable hypotheses, 270, 321

Ideas that come to author's mind, 19, 76
    Suggestions of others, 83-84
Illustrative materials, 305-314
Implications, 323
Independent variable, 131
Index, 328
Ink work, 311
Instruments, 98-99, 296
Interlibrary loan service, 54
Internal validity, 20, 90
Interviewer, 98-99, 167
Interviews, 168-183
    Tape recording, 173, 182
Introduction
    Of proposal, 31-33
    Of final study, 266-274
Introductory statements, 357, 360
Italics, 496-500
Items in series, 391-395

Leaders, 501-502
Letters requesting information, 134-138
Library helps, 52-54
Limiting the problem, 14-16

Machine tabulating and scoring, 157, 198

National Union catalog, 54
Notes on bibliography cards, 62-66
Notes on content cards, 58
    Quotations, 69-74
Note-taking cards, 67-77
Numbered bibliography, 289
Numbering
    In numbered bibliography, 289
    Of chapters, 240
    Of division and subdivision headings, 343
    Of figures, 308
    Of footnotes, 286, 289
    Of tables, 308
Numbers, 475-477

Observation, 184-189
    Tape recording, 189

Omissions in quotations, 70, 277
"Open" questions, 146
Opinionnaires, 145-161
   Directions, 150
Organization of study, 22
Outline
   Preliminary, 21-25
   First draft, 236-248

Paragraph structure, 356, 359, 362-371
Parallel construction, 390
Paraphrasing, 282
Parentheses, 504-508
Pencil-and-paper instruments, 139-144
Period, 509-511
Permission to use, 94-96
   For interview, 175
   Quoted material, 281
Personal comment or opinion, 262-263, 302
Philosophical research, 113
Pilot study, 88, 106
   Of interview, 173
   Of questionnaire, 160
Planning the study, 17-50
   Writing a preliminary outline, 21-25
   Writing a proposal, 26-50
Plurals, 451-456
Possessives, 413-415, 457-461
Preliminary outline, 21-25
Prepositions, 396
Pronouns, 406-412
Proofread final copy, 350
Proposal, 26-59
Punctuation, 482-526
   Brackets, 484-486
   Colon, 487-490
   Comma, 491-492
   Dash, 493-494
   Exclamation point, 495
   Italics, 496-500
   Leaders, 501-502
   Parentheses, 503-508
   Period, 509-511
   Question mark, 512-514
   Quotation marks, 515-523
   Semicolon, 524-526

Quasi-experimental studies, 88, 227, 232
Question mark, 512-514
Questionnaires, 145-161
   Arrangement of questions, 151
   "Closed" questions, 146
   Directions, 150
   "Open" questions, 146
   Pilot study, 160
   Preparation for IBM punching, 157
   Structure of questions, 153-155
Quotation marks, 515-523
Quotations
   In first draft, 277-282
   In note-taking, 69-74
   Inserting your own words, 72
   Permission to quote, 281
   Use of "sic," 71

Reading extensively, 51-80
Recommendations, 322-323
Reference guides, 52-54
Reliability, 47, 91, 165, 194, 196
Research
   Descriptive, 114-128
   Experimental, 129-133
   Historical, 109-113
   Research in general, 81-108
Research problem, 8-13
Review of related research
   In proposal, 34
   In study, 275-276
Revising the report, 329-352
Rhetoric, 353-371

Sampling, 88
Scoring procedures, 102, 104-105
Seek criticism, 346-347
Semicolon, 524-526
Sentence structure, 356, 360, 372-389
Series, 391-395
Spelling, 446-477
Sponsorship for study, 11
Standardized tests and other measuring devices, 162-167
Statistical procedures, 103-104, 200-203, 217-218, 297, 314
Status studies, 120
Style manual, 349
Style of manuscript, 264
   Of bibliography, 325
   Of tabular material, 307
   Of typed copy, 349
Style sheet, 446-447
Summary of study, 317-318, 352
Supplementary pages, 324-328
   Appendix, 327
   Bibliography, 324-326
   Index, 328
Surveys, 120-124
Symbols for notes, 287

Synonyms, 437, 440
Tables, 234-235, 305-313
   Form, 307
   In appendix, 308
   Include in first draft, 305
   Numbering, 308
   Titles, 310
Taking notes, 6, 58-77
   Bibliography cards, 62-66
   Filing notes, 78-80
   Multicopying notes, 60
   Note-taking cards, 67-77
   Organizing and reviewing cards, 260
Tape recording
   Interviews, 183
   Observations, 189
   Pilot study, 173
Technical terms, 45, 100-101, 200, 274
Tests, 158-164
   Administration, 167
   Directions, 165
Thinking through the problem, 256-265
Title
   Of chapters, 240
   Of figures, 310
   Of proposal, 27
   Of study, 256, 333
   Of tables, 310
Tools, 93, 97, 116
Topic, selection of, 1-13
Topic sentences, 363-364
Transition statements, 358, 369-370
Typing final copy, 349
   Revised material, 345

Unity, 356

Validity, 20, 47, 90-91, 165, 194, 196, 208
Variables
   Independent, 127
   Dependent, 127
Verb form, 416-434
   Gerunds, 431, 434
   Infinitives, 431-432
   Mood, 429-430
   Number, 417-426
   Participles, 431, 433
   Tense, 427
   Voice, 428
Vocabulary, 435-445

Working conditions, 249-255
Writing the report, 236-352

A MANUAL OF FORM FOR
THESES AND TERM REPORTS

(Third Revision, 1967)

by KATHLEEN DUGDALE

A detailed and carefully indexed manual of form for typewritten materials, including rules for footnotes, quotations, tables, figures, bibliography, etc. Contains many pages of examples.

(Available at the Indiana University Bookstore, Bloomington)